Alberto Pinto
Text by Julien Morel

# ALBERTO PINTO
# TODAY

Flammarion

# Contents

Readers opening this book for the first time and turning its pages are entering the marvelous world of Alberto Pinto.

"Blessed with gifts," Alberto is a friend. And, though his sole ambition is to produce good work, he is now a celebrity the world over. Fame has had no discernible effect on his personality, however, and he remains, as always, considerate, poised, and immensely kind.

An interior design magician, he turns the most extraordinary dreams into reality, creating settings that maintain that delicate balance between decorative delight and excess.

As the work of an interior designer is necessarily ephemeral—wealthy clients often change their decor—this volume preserves for the future an image of what has become a unique style: at once classic and modern, luxurious and yet in step with its time, and above all obsessed with perfection.

From a haute couture airplane to a 220-foot yacht, from a New York apartment to a country house in England, these interiors live and breathe in the same exciting yet inimitable atmosphere: "The Pinto Touch."

François de Ricqlès
Chairman, Christie's France

Facing page When Alberto Pinto decorated this former farmhouse in La Palmeraie of Marrakech, converted into a holiday home in the twentieth century, he drew his inspiration from the rich trove of Moroccan objects and techniques, and combined them with European tastes and habits. As shown in this bedroom, the oriental tone cultivated throughout the house is neither ethnographic, nor romantic, but simply contemporary. On the finely sculpted cedar desk, a breath of the lverdant park is gathered up in the freshly picked bouquet that hints at the colors of the textiles and the choice of Central Asian *suzani* fabric used as a bed throw.

Alberto Pinto was born French, but in a foreign land; his home was an exotic otherness, featuring Casablanca and Tangier as the first ports of call. It was idyllic, sun-drenched scenery in which to grow up and a starting-point for the countless journeys that studded his cosmopolitan childhood. He traveled frequently to Paris—where his childhood house served as a true embassy—and regularly throughout the world, which he began exploring at a very young age in the company of his inquisitive parents, who loved to travel. A natural globe-trotter even today, the interior designer skillfully harnesses these influences and his enlightened eclecticism to embody the excellence of the "French Touch" to decorative art. From his headquarters at the Hôtel de la Victoire in Paris, he coordinates projects of impressive scale in all four corners of the planet. The exclusive terminal of an airport at Doha; the largest private residence in New York; many thousand square feet for a home in London; "super-yachts" more than three hundred feet long; private aircraft; office buildings; the prestigious Hôtel Lambert, widely considered as the finest private mansion in Paris; the Hôtel Pozzo di Borgo; and the sublime Hôtel Kinski are all current commissions.

The creativity and diversity of Alberto Pinto's plans are no less striking than their sheer magnitude. In revealing some of the most recent projects to the public, *Alberto Pinto Today* provides a sense of their breadth. Not for twenty years had a volume encompassed the entire spectrum of an oeuvre that had instead been presented in typological fragments. Volumes such as *Classics, Corporate, Orientalism, Bedrooms,* and *Table Settings*—published by Flammarion and by Rizzoli—thus focus on a specific theme, teasing out Alberto Pinto's admirable faculty for regenerating the history of the international style, constantly surprising us while respecting established codes.

The decorative agendas realized by Alberto Pinto are in keeping with the often exceptional lifestyles of his patrons: the exclusive preserve of a restricted number of art-lovers, collectors, high-flying executives, crowned heads, and A-list companies, whose overriding imperative is for something utterly unique, each project is a private or public microcosm.

To satisfy such demands, Alberto Pinto's projects deliberately eschew the narcissistic temptation to impose his own taste, steering clear of rigid historicism and provocative avant-gardism alike. He simply turns his customers' dreams into realizable plans. A brief conversation and acquaintance with a few objects provides him with enough material for an interior designed to reflect a culture, a way of life, and an imagination, which together serve as the backdrop to a uniquely distinctive lifestyle.

A thumbnail biographical sketch may cast some light on this extraordinary ability to keep abreast of so much at once. Firstly, an innate inquisitiveness is aided and abetted by his phenomenal memory. After a childhood spent in some of the most beautiful places on earth, he went on to study art history in the footsteps of Proust at the École du Louvre. Then came a period in New York in the sixties, reporting on the finest contemporary interiors for Condé Nast, followed by a debut project for himself that played a key role in his trajectory, just as a catwalk launch does for a great couturier. Perhaps it was fate after all, but Alberto Pinto thus by chance found himself at the summit of the interior decorating world. After a breakthrough commission for Mrs. Rosemarie Kanzler at Saint-Jean-Cap-Ferrat, his name was soon being uttered in hushed tones as the man responsible for a titanic realization, whose style defies fashion and has lost none of its gloss over time.

Mastering any number of foreign languages (he speaks six without ever consciously studying them), as he does all the idioms of interior decoration, Alberto Pinto possesses an encyclopedic knowledge of the arts and their techniques, though he is instinctively always on the lookout for more.

A tireless eye records every detail of his environment, as if photographically. A film set, the ambience of a house, the finish on a fashion accessory or a piece of clothing, the layout of a book or a sale catalog, a scrap of cloth or piece of embroidery are all grist to his mill, filed away, lying dormant in his unconscious, ready to surge forth in the ongoing genesis of a new project.

**Facing page** The decoration of the magnificently stocked library, which extends over two floors of this North American holiday home, had three guiding elements: an eclectic array of twentieth-century shapes, a welcoming ambience, and an opening onto the garden. The space is entirely paneled in walnut wood and made distinctive by the monumental stone fireplace, which is several feet high. The furniture and objects brought together in the room display Albert Pinto's mastery of style and decorative languages.

Meanwhile, Alberto Pinto's sixty collaborators act as guardians of his vision: day after day, these architects, interior designers, project supervisors, stylists, technical draughtsmen, researchers, etc., work tirelessly to turn Alberto Pinto's plans into a living reality. It is crucial that every project allows the space it occupies to breathe; Alberto Pinto's interiors encourage the body to be comfortable. Imperceptibly—as if someone were being asked to sit, to stand straighter—both line and ornament, spurred on by an interplay between materials (some precious, some less exalted) and their texture, make one more alert; if the artworks and objects assembled arouse our curiosity and beguile the eye, it is the pure colors and the sharpness of the counterpoint that preclude monotony. Down to the very least detail—be it the evenness of a saddle-stitch, an artistic table setting, or some quality linen—the environments signed by Maison Alberto Pinto are all demonstrations of a certain idea of luxury, where comfort reigns unobtrusively, providing a framework for exceptional lives.

The creative brio of the Hôtel de la Victoire, a forcing-ground where each unique project can germinate, testifies to a constant striving for excellence and improvement. There, each collaborator has his or her valid contribution to make. Preferring to guide rather than to spoon-feed, Alberto Pinto radiates a serenity, an energy that spurs on the many talents that have coalesced around him to give their virtuosity free rein.

Predicated on craftsmanship and expertise, many factors offer constant stimulation to the climate of innovation in this bureau, heir apparent to the venerable French tradition of interior decoration: *objets d'art* snapped up from auction houses or antique dealers the world over; a library endowed with several hundred volumes; a selection of more than eight thousand swatches of fabric; a materials collection ready to solve every conceivable decorative dilemma; and a growing databank of more than five thousand suppliers.

Embroiderers, tapestry-makers, staffers, bronze-casters, cabinet-makers, carpenters, painters, and sculptors are among the skills pooled by Alberto Pinto's agency, adding the craftmanship and essence of traditional guilds. It is these valuable team members who give concrete form to the perspective drawings and 3-D mock-ups presented to clients early on in the process—compositions where at least a third will be pure creation and which are all formulated in accordance with the extremely precise indications of Alberto Pinto.

Hervé Van der Straeten, Stephan Mocanu, Lenka Beillevert, and Dominique Derive are just some of the names from the network of loyal artists who employ their talent to achieve the vision of the international decorator.

If one asks him today for the secret behind a method that has led to forty years of success, Alberto Pinto first mentions the seriousness with which the client's desires must be treated, going on to evoke the importance of psychology, consideration, expeditiousness, and rigor in defining and realizing them. The development of a project, then, starts by listening; gradually, Alberto Pinto draws up the guidelines for a composition in which he will place—but never impose—his palette. If the idiom is rooted in a grammar of space of which he is a preeminent master, its decorative vocabulary is simply inexhaustible. An avowed eclecticism meets with a sense of coherence. It is from this that emanates the *genius loci*, but without losing the hallmarks of a brand, bringing to the international interior design scene those unmistakable signs of typically French luxury for which Alberto Pinto acts as a tireless ambassador.

He represents this luxury notably through his brand Pinto Paris, which has recently furthered the exclusiveness of his fine dining ware with the release of a debut furniture collection christened "Rio." Using carefully selected original creations from his workshops, it celebrates the genius of applied arts and daring combinations of materials, all devoted to the service of comfort and elegance.

In the two showrooms now open by appointment at the Hôtel de la Victoire, enlightened enthusiasts can find part of the dreams materialized in interiors whose prodigious vitality is amply illustrated in the following pages.

Contemporary loft spaces, historic reworkings of fine residences, houses by the sea, or European farms in the palm plantations of Marrakech; but also office buildings, "super-yachts," and private jets—the projects revealed in this book prove that nothing can limit Alberto Pinto's talent. Never freer than when resolving fresh challenges and defining intimacy in large spaces, he awakens the spirit of each place where the creative and the original reign supreme.

---

**Facing page** In Paris, in between flights, Alberto Pinto gives himself over to this portrait with characteristic amiability. His smile and intense gaze reinforce his sympathetic traits, while a slight movement reveals his impatience to break the pose. A busy man, more at home observing others than indulging in self-display, this indefatigable ambassador of fine French interior decoration, Chevalier des Arts et des Lettres, and Commandeur de la Légion d'Honneur infinitely prefers discretion to the limelight.

# Private Collection in London

nterior decoration is a younger brother of art, and usually thought of as far less profound. Yet, if considered and carefully constructed, it can reveal a rich sense of personal history. In fact, the way objects are arranged in a house, the manner in which they mutually enhance each other can express a spirit, as well as a particular walk of life: this ability is all the more perceptible when it functions as the backdrop to the life of a couple that collects art. Located in the heart of London, this home is owned by two lovers of modern and contemporary painting who possess a collection including many large pieces, together with Asian antiquities. Confronted, when they purchased the house, with an outdated and fragmented room layout, they turned to Alberto Pinto, whose visual intelligence they had already had cause to appreciate on many occasions. He transformed the spaces where he preserved only the shell: freeing its volumes to the full, the entire interior ensemble radiates from a centrally placed hub. The ebony-colored doorframes, extending to the full height of the walls, arrange the perspectives of each room so that the space is unified, as in a loft. It is an approach that, if it creates a spacious sense of grandeur, also allows it to be structured.

The aesthetic impact of the collection—boasting signatures such as Francis Bacon, Gerhard Richter, and Max Ernst—can only benefit from the understated approach: surrounded by the purest lines, the art is left free to work its full effect. The white stucco, fabric, straw, or braided wood marquetry on the walls allow one's attention to be attracted to the art. Similarly, furnishing fabrics in raw cotton keep it in the limelight, emphasizing moreover the quality of the embroidery trim. Some are redolent of patterns on a *tsuba* (a decorative hilt in Japanese weaponry), a set of which appears here, together with other fine ornaments of Asian civilization. Featuring valuable pieces of furniture and cleverly deployed folding screens, the decor enters into spontaneous dialog with the representatives of contemporary abstraction. Far Eastern rigor also informs the calm unfussiness of the interior, creating a favorable climate for aesthetic receptivity where ornament is restricted to "sculptural" furniture drawn in clear, crisp lines. Modern but never chilly, this *japonisant* atmosphere once again comes to the fore in the master bedroom. Lined with silk and set off with crackled red lacquer calpinage—an assemblage that can also be composed of marble, stone, terracotta, etc.—the walls evoke the traditional partitions of a distant Orient. They form a superb setting for the folding screen that, in an audacious arrangement, conceals the access to the dressing room. Once again, the decor acts as a majestic backdrop to an artistic masterpiece. Indeed, perhaps Alberto Pinto's consummate genius resides in a gift for sublimation.

**Facing page and above** The longest stretch of wall in the lounge is occupied floor to ceiling by a Gerhard Richter canvas. Opposite, a Bacon looks down on an ample and deep-set settee covered in simple white cotton embroidered with a haphazard pattern of cherry-ripe *tsuba* motifs. Behind the two art deco armchairs, two varnished console tables with fine gilt ornamentation contribute to the *japonisant* atmosphere that infuses the whole plan. Like all the furniture in the apartment, the imposing low table, signed Hervé Van der Straeten, is a work of art in itself.

**Facing page** As if lifted from Gerhard Richter's painting, light touches of color give life to the spare lines of the decor. Thus the striking effect of the canvas is extended into the space by nuances such as the embroidery on the raw cottoncovered settees and curtains, or the orange stem of the lamp standing on a bronze Japanese-style side table. Such bright hues stand out against the studied neutrality of an interior dedicated to natural materials. The light-colored coir effect woolen fitted carpet and the straw on the walls bring out the best in the collection and enhance some opulent pieces of furniture such as this bronze footstool by Hervé Van der Straeten that is as much a sculpture as a seat. The wild grace of orchids offers an elegant counterpoint to the atmosphere.

Facing page and right A tea set designed
by Alberto Pinto is arranged behind
a vintage Japanese folding screen.
It is embellished with an allusively graphic
coral pattern harmonizing with the delicate
gold calligraphy that stands out against
the richness of the lacquer. Here practicality
is astutely combined with aesthetics and
the screen panels are in fact unexpectedly
functional: encased in structures made
of bronze they serve as doors for a wall
cupboard invisible to the uninitiated. Indeed,
when the doors are shut it is impossible
to tell that the piece possesses this dual
personality. This eye-catching screen is the
showpiece of the dining-room decor.
The material of the contemporary chandelier
suspended over the table echoes the
delicate motifs emerging from the black
lacquer back ground. The chairs with their
slim backs add a touch of solemnity to the
Zen-like design.

**Facing page and left** A non-continuous partition joins the television room to the corridor, with a broad frame signaling the division that allows another canvas by Gerhard Richter to come into its own. The walls in this room are lined with braided wood, affording a marvelous contrasting effect with the painting. The two comfortable couches covered in natural white cotton are enough to furnish a space relieved by some leather scatter cushions. The view down the corridor offers a rewarding glimpse of the linear language of the whole interior. As if balanced on a ring, the slimline top of an eminently contemporary console table stretches along the wall. The same visual zest recurs in the staircase, whose transparent glass balustrade allows visitors to enjoy the interplay between the supple lines of the undulating guardrail and the severe rectilinear sawtooth of the steps, not forgetting the interestingly-shaped armchair nestling under the stairway.

**Left** The reconfiguration of the interior space has liberated sufficient volume for an office in which a vast Gerhard Richter flexes its ample form. In order to feast one's eyes on this, a gloriously comfortable armchair with footstool has been placed in front of the picture. To the rear, the study boasts a dark-wood bookcase with glass shelving designed by Alberto Pinto. Behind the desk, a small Max Ernst more than holds its own against the limewashed white stucco wall.

**Right** The elegant sobriety presiding over the entire installation is pursued in the guest quarters, where the neutral materials are but punctuated by touches of gray: a band of fabric laid on the bedspread meets a few cushions, while the lampshades take up the predominant tone of the two abstract paintings signed Zao Wou Ki. The two compartments either side of the bed-head hold Japanese lacquer boxes, while the pendant lamps were designed by Alberto Pinto's office. In a pale wood rimmed in dark, the master dressing room is a functional, light-filled space encapsulating the rigorous and individual design that is the hallmark of any Alberto Pinto interior.

**Facing page** In the guest bathroom, the huge mirrors that multiply the space to infinity are encased in black Portoro marble.

**Left and facing page** In the master bedroom, the walls lined in light-hued coarse silk are decorated with crackled red calpinage reminiscent of the partitions in traditional Japanese houses. The same fabric is employed for the curtains, while the side chairs and footstools are covered in a dotted floral pattern that recurs on the bed-head, which is flanked by two bronze and lacquer bedside tables in the Jansen taste. Behind the large Chinese folding screen, a hidden alcove has been converted into a dressing room. As in the dining room, this sleight of hand not only emphasizes the beauty of a venerable room, it also provides an intelligent and unexpected functional twist.

**Facing page** For a client from abroad who, when in Paris, wants to savor the quintessence of the French spirit, Alberto Pinto returns to the time-honored traditions of the neoclassical style. Already altered on several occasions, the ample volumes of this Haussmann apartment lend themselves marvelously to a new decor worthy of the most splendid private abodes. Parquet flooring, molding, stone, and painted woodwork are the *sine qua non* in this type of project, which presents the additional challenge of having to accommodate a first-rate collection of contemporary art.

For Alberto Pinto, though, what might look like a constraint is magically transformed into an opportunity to display a total mastery of contrast and eclecticism. This is confirmed as early as the entrance hall, where an antique bust finds itself in the company of a powerful red nude, a juxtaposition further heightened by the classicism of the marquetry flooring, an antiquity-inspired Empire chandelier, a Louis XV chair, but also by a door surround enlivened by the carved stucco laurel garland and ornamental brazier in the overdoor.

# Classical Decor
# for Contemporary Art

Under Alberto Pinto's watchful eye, an ample Paris apartment chosen as a pied-à-terre by a foreign businessman finds its roots in the authenticity of the classical. The client's desire was to recapture something of the refinement of the French Grand Siècle, into which was integrated a prestigious array of contemporary artworks. This commission allowed the designer to display the characteristic flavor of his work. Each juxtaposition participates in the unmistakable, highly individual world to which Alberto Pinto is so attached. His creativity allows him to break free of the doctrinal straitjacket of the classical, letting a taste for things past inform the present and add to the pleasure of each passing day. To situate this daring art collection within a typically eighteenth-century framework thus became an aesthetic challenge, rather like those blockbuster exhibitions in which avant-garde works are hung in a period setting. Paintings and sculptures signed Jan Fabre, Arman, Dan Flavin, Luciano Fontana, Anish Kapoor, and Wim Delvoye, as well as pieces of Concorde acquired on the airliner's decommissioning, hold their own against the neoclassical patina and rigor. A discreet antique bust draws the eye away from an abstract nude. The metallic green wings of the beetles in a piece by Jan Fabre enliven the white wooden paneling—a foil to the quality of its gilding. A spinal column by the same artist becomes a sculpture that, arranged between two windows, underlines the rhythmic verticals of the molding. It is hard to believe that this entire decor, replacing the original ornaments in their architectural setting, is in fact an invention. Mistreated in the course of ill-advised renovation work in the eighties, the apartment had completely lost its original face. Art and authenticity are equally instrumental in its restoration: the stone, the marquetry flooring, the woodwork, the painted dados, woodwork, and doors, and the delicacy of the carving by classical *ornamentistes* all conspire in a backdrop that sets off the grace of the bijou furniture found on the antique market or else recreated to the scale of the rooms and following the rules of the style to the letter. Soft furnishings cheer up the window surrounds, while couches and armchairs are covered and trimmed with precious fabrics.

Lying at the heart of this classical composition, the contemporary art brings with it surprise and buoyancy. Like the convex mirror by Anish Kapoor, in which the view of the drawing room is reversed, the art's reconciled contradictions ask questions of the eye. The contemporary and the classical enhance each other in an oxymoron typical of Paris, a city where bustling creative energy has always had to vie with the magnificence of the past.

**Pages 26–27** In terms of decoration, the drawing room is tailor-made for the classical manner: the straight lines of the fine gilded woodwork framing the uncluttered tables, like the half moon overdoors, are directly inspired by the Louis XVI style of the later eighteenth century. Heavy and thick, the curtains lined in blue silk embroidered with white plant motifs tumble down before the lofty windows from elaborate gilded metal runners and are held in place by beautifully made tiebacks. Beneath a chandelier delicately hung with glass droplets, the furniture associates antique and contemporary in a fusion of today's lifestyle and yesteryear's aesthetic.

**Facing page and left** On the paneling in the drawing room, a convex mirror by Anish Kapoor whisks us back in time. It brings out the paradoxical timelessness of Alberto Pinto's reinterpretation of the classical style. Lucio Fontana's slashed canvases between two windows or, above a desk unearthed at an antique dealer's, the picture delicately covered in beetle wings by Jan Fabre also take their cue from this fruitful amalgam of different eras. A corner able to serve four diners opens into the kitchen. The parquet flooring, the elegant fireplace and rear wall mirror framed in fine gilt molding bring a wealth of refinement.
Under a cloche standing next to two Sèvres vases, the *mise en abyme* of the surrealist relief by René Magritte introduces a soupçon of irony, while a carbonized wooden bas-relief by Evers provides a further example of historical interplay.

**Facing page** The table in the large dining room is grandly laid beneath a chandelier dripping with crystal. The art of the table occupies a privileged place in the Alberto Pinto universe. His global view of interior design means that projects bristle with details and accessories that make everyday life an unforgettable experience. Here we have the "Parrots—Yellow Brazil" service, a refined composition hand-painted on fine Limoges porcelain. Bohemian crystal completes an unfussy but sophisticated table setting. In front of the pier glass surmounted by an overmantel emblazoned with *grotteschi*, a relic from the Concorde sits between two candelabra. The hardstone vases on the piers, meanwhile, like the grotesque motif hand-painted on the door panels, rewrite the language of French classicism in today's idiom.

**Above** Around the table, the scroll-back chairs already lean toward the Empire style, demonstrating Alberto Pinto's flexibility in composing these stylistic symphonies. Their gilded carving perfectly echoes the coving, molding, and dado panels illustrated with grotesques. The works on the walls offer a more contemporary counterpoint, including a sculpture by Lucio Fontana and a sizable canvas by Manolo Valdès.

**Left** In the corridor leading to one of
the smaller rooms, the blinds set the scene
for an original decor inspired by old
architectural drawings. The composition
recurs above the plain wood carving
in the room itself, forming a welcoming and
more informal nest. The small framed work
leaning against the window beneath
the fabric blinds is signed Max Ernst.
The pyramidal feet of the coffee table and
the side table refer back to the neoclassical
style, whereas the deep accommodating
settees are more in keeping with twentieth-
century standards of comfort.

**Facing page** This guest bathroom—with its
painted *trompe l'oeil* marquetry decor—is a
veritable masterpiece. The choice of a metal
hand-basin in a dark marble surround, with
the gilt bronze taps and fittings, continues
the vein of a neoclassicism that is prepared
to rub shoulders with the more up-to-date.

**Above and facing page** Awash with sunlight, the generous volumes of the master bathroom make for what is in essence a vast bathing hall. In the neoclassical manner, a large round swing mirror gazes down on the basin and its marble surround, reflecting an enigmatic if uncompromising composition by the lens of photographer Thomas Ruth. The pale blue bedroom respects the sobriety of the Louis XVI style, the arched mirror at the top of the bed framed by two typical neoclassical grooved pilasters rudented (their flutings filled) with asparagus motifs. Reflected in the foreground stands a sculpture by Arman entitled *The Chessboard*, while on the rear wall hangs an X-ray piece by Belgian artist Wim Delvoye. The whole project presents a prime example of how a master of eclecticism like Alberto Pinto can deploy the rigor and sobriety of neoclassicism to set off a first-rate collection of contemporary art. The ease with which he reconciles opposites and overcomes constraints creates an impressive ensemble at once heterogenous and in harmony.

**Facing page** The standards Alberto Pinto sets when dealing with the service sector are on much the same level as for a deluxe hotel. His elaborate yet coherent visual touches applied to a reception hall or to a system of horizontal and vertical flows can make sense of the most unwieldy volumes. In this reception hall, they are centered on a thorough program of research on material and texture, and on the deployment of furniture of a sculptural aspect. Conceived in total harmony with the architecture, the keynote to the decor is provided by the sinuous lines of the façade, while the daylight is treated as fluid and plays a full part in the ornamental program. On the floor, an inlaid aluminum band echoes the great circular light well beneath which coils the undulating shape of a pair of vast benches. Up on the ceiling, meanwhile, aluminum foil cladding diffuses a silvery shimmer.

# Curves on the Bank of the Seine

The HRO River Ouest Program is the most recent "corporate" contract the Maison Alberto Pinto has delivered. Located in the "Bord de Seine," a new business quarter on the fringes of Paris, it conducts a fruitful collaboration with the American Howard Ronson, founder of the HRO group. The eighties encounter between these two visionaries marked the advent of a total revolution in office fitting and installation. Adopting as his own Robert Loewy's motto "ugliness sells badly," it was Howard Ronson who first realized that the negotiation of a real estate project went more smoothly when it featured quality interiors. This consideration provided Alberto Pinto with an opportunity to embark on an exercise in which he has proved himself especially adroit. The challenge was to create a formula adapted to space planning and services in the context of constructions of vast size.

Still topical, the solutions adopted by Alberto Pinto have become paragons of the genre. With a strong and forward-looking vision, he maximizes the reception space, humanizes the vertical and horizontal axes of flow, deploying quality finishes and trim, plus superior materials, in conjunction with works of art. The atmosphere in the staff canteen is no longer soulless; meanwhile, auditoriums, and conference and meeting-rooms. are conducive to concentration and calm, encouraged by a supremely elegant layout.

Particularly at ease with larger volumes, Alberto Pinto embraces the space completely: he handles gigantism with virtuosity, imparting structure to the void by the rational use of certain key components, the linchpins of his design layout. Sobriety and modernity enhance the image of the business, while, in parallel, comfort and harmony fosters well-being among its employees. The 194,000 square feet (18,000 square meters) of the HRO River Ouest submitted for design (out of a total of 730,000 square feet, 68,000 square meters) amount in fact to a restatement of the brief, reinterpreted in a manner that underlines the structure. The dynamic of the entire project derives from curved lines, evoking as much the notion of the free flow of ideas and information as the bank of the River Seine on which the complex is built.

The river fronts initiate a rhythm that is extended in the mineral and vegetal ova designed in tandem with landscape designer Eric Ciborowski, becoming the sum and substance of the interior's entire agenda: aluminum fillets set into the floor; hypnotically curving benches-cum-sculptures; ceilings adorned with metal leaf; the loose lines animating the wood-paneled corridors…. If the whole project bears the stamp of adaptability, this is amplified by the deployment of innovative materials and by textures tailor-made for the site.

Whereas the zones are composed with fluidity, the large auditorium and the work-rooms opt for a sober and poised sense of comfort. By contrast color and suppleness resurface in the zestful and energizing staff restaurants. The ensemble distills a contemporary image of an intelligence—and communication—led industry that will be the focus of business in the century to come.

**Facing page and left** The HRO River Ouest complex includes three receptions distinguished by the color of the upholstered bench in the center. The reception desk with its fluid lines was conceived by Maison Alberto Pinto specifically for this project. The formal elegance of this jigsaw puzzle comprising fifty pieces of Corian® is extrapolated in the powerful graphics of the stucco fresco composed according to recommendations from Alberto Pinto by the artist Lenka Beillevert. Conforming to the spirit of elegant sobriety that governs the entire contract, geometric forms, material effects, and a toned-down palette ranging from creamy white via various shades of gray beige animate the wall. The vitrified stoneware tiles are given added prestige through various finishes exclusively devised for the site, while aluminum incrustations reproduce on the floor the structural forms that give the ceiling its rewarding individuality. Dressed with aluminum leaf, the shape evokes an air bubble trapped beneath some imaginary ice sheet. The sanded glass walls were also an innovation developed and perfected in response to Alberto Pinto's vision. The same design is stamped into the metal on the elevator doors. The elevators themselves, all glass (plain and mirror) and metal, subscribe to the pervasive dynamic of technical brio made audible by the descant of a contemporary decor in total symbiosis with the architecture.

**Facing page and right** The contours
of the corridors leading to the meeting
and conference rooms fitted out by Alberto
Pinto exude the muted atmosphere
of an antechamber. This comfortable and
understated luxury is aided and abetted by
the choice of materials used to differentiate
the various zones. Tall, slender torchère wall
lights protrude at regular intervals from the
wood lining the undulating wall. Elsewhere,
carved wood panels enliven vertical surfaces
distinguished by an informed and careful
selection of contemporary artworks.
Long console tables and lunar bracket
lamps along the walls enhance the surface.
Comfortable lounges are the perfect
backdrop to a dialog between equals.
Designer furniture combined with pieces
specially envisaged for the structure make
for a cozy yet modern atmosphere.

**Pages 42–43** From this vast atrium radiate
services for the whole complex. Beneath
a gigantic suspension lamp—a levitating
light-cum-UFO—two armchairs fulfill
a sculptural role. As if squaring up to one
another, these two marvels of design
announce the purpose of a building devoted
to meetings and conferences, but which
is also a place for relaxation appointed
with several restaurants, lounges, and sports
halls to cater for the wellbeing of all the
associates of the companies located here.

**Facing page and right** A 150-seat
amphitheater offers a comfortable and
cordial venue for large-scale conferences.
Exceeding the usual standards in the service
sector, the seating is leather upholstered.
Retractable tray-tables are incorporated into
the armrests for rapid note-taking. Boasting
diamond-patterned wood veneer panels with
tubes between the joints that cross and emit
a blue-tinged light, the abiding atmosphere
is one of a gloriously lavish movie theater.
This story presents multipurpose conference
rooms that open out into the garden.
The same color scheme is found in
a combination of dark wood and straw
marquetry lining the wall, a beige fitted
carpet, and chairs with orange leather seats
and white leather backs. The light metal
feet of the tables and armchairs translate
the fluidity and sobriety of the space.

**Facing page and right** The site is provided with two eating facilities laid out according to identical principles but strongly differentiated by a contrasting palette. Whereas in one royal blue predominates, the other is ruled by an energizing orange. In both cases, the visual effect is enlivened by the sinuous ebb and flow of the Panton seats set around the tables and the optical pattern on the carpet. The dynamism and vitality of the interior is in step with the conviviality of collective eating. The decorative script for the lounge bar that opens through to the terrace allots a starring role to design, promoting an atmosphere conducive to informal after-work get-togethers. The voluptuous contours of the shining black bar set up a striking contrast with the white stools, while the light- and dark-wood marquetry on the wall echoes the wave motif that often recurs in this 194,000 square foot (18,000 square meter) project completely unified by the penetrating vision of Alberto Pinto.

# Hostellerie de Plaisance at Saint-Émilion

Alberto Pinto seldom takes on hotel interiors. In general, he prefers private homes, more conducive to the expression of his approach to decoration. However, at Saint-Émilion he did agree to direct the renovation of the Hostellerie de Plaisance, a Relais et Châteaux hotel with seventeen rooms and four suites, whose proportions allowed him to give free expression to his flair for detail and personalization.

Positively exuding history, the place offered a heaven-sent opportunity to tear up the rule-book: here, standardization and monotony were out of the question and are successfully banished by Pinto's breathtaking talent for making the best of an exceptional site, rooted in a landscape that is the result of the gifts of nature combining with human passion. A UNESCO world heritage site, the *terroir*, the very soil of Saint-Émilion was transformed by Alberto Pinto into fertile ground for his design approach; tapping into the characteristic limestone of the land, into its color and spirit, in a plan in which authenticity is wedded to inventiveness, he crystallizes the very essence of a truly remarkable location.

Split over two sites—an ancient cloister perched at the top of the village and an ancestral house down the slope—the hotel is unified by the interior designer's overall vision. In interpreting its topographic complexity, he has spun an extended metaphor for the hill and the quaint village nestling at its flank. The main building and its annex are connected by a series of hanging gardens and an underground glass elevator cut into the rock—the ultimate refined variation on the region's venerable troglodyte tradition.

Perfectly integrated into the original edifice, the reception hall was carved out from the square in the upper village, thereby allowing Alberto Pinto to clarify and reassign its various zones. As the square proudly bears the imprint of a history it would be insolent to want to mimic, the tone is set by a resolutely contemporary reception desk. With a nod to the surrounding vineyards, the leather-lined drawing room, with tawny as the dominant color, is awash with the hues of autumn. In this cordial, subdued environment, one can linger for hours over a cup of tea or one last drink. Like tracery in the sunlight, the restaurant (having earned a second Michelin star since the works were done) turns its face towards the shimmering village.

Up in the bedrooms, the standards of comfort are American, though the atmosphere takes its cue from England. All have generously appointed bathrooms (a natural extension of the notion of wellbeing), but otherwise the graphic details and colors in each room afford a personal touch.

Combining craft at its most compelling with a timely appreciation of the picturesque revived in precincts as hallowed as they are irregular, Alberto Pinto captures the essence of a region that puts its trust in sharing and hospitality. A stylized vine trail in fresco, the names of each of the proprietor's vineyards engraved into the wall remind us never to forget that we are standing atop a *terroir*—on land dedicated to welcoming and to perpetuating its own deathless memory.

**Facing page and left** Alberto Pinto's initial intervention in the project was architectural, redefining the zones to create more harmonious flows throughout the hotel and imparting dynamism to the space. The former bar was transformed into a restaurant room with large windows that open on to the terrace. Enhanced by original woodwork simply treated with white lead, the nobility of the volume has the feel of a baronial hall in which the candles in the wrought-iron chandeliers seem to diffuse a glow from the dawn of history. The yellow overstitched embroidery on the thick drapes and on the fabric chosen for the armchairs and table cover refracts the solar energy of the incoming light. Hung with a decidedly modern ceiling light, the corridor to the right leads to the restaurant cloakrooms. On the floor, the large paving stones are enlivened with cabochons of eighteenth-century inspiration. The space is furnished by a chair and a bench picked up on the antique market, while the mock-stone cladding on the walls is inscribed with the names of all the vineyards belonging to the proprietor of the hotel in a subtle invitation to explore the region and sample its wines.

**Pages 52–53** Two old wrought-iron wine-cellar gates lead through into the fawn-colored nest of the hotel bar, enwrapped in an autumnal hue. The tangible warmth of this room plainly emanates from the leather squares on the walls, hand cut and individually placed in position. Their caramel tonality feels in perfect harmony with the orangy red of the embroidery decorating the heavy curtains and the fabric on the cushions and armchairs, and it even reappears in dots on the faux leopard fitted carpet.

**Facing page and left** Allergic to repetition, Alberto Pinto has given each room in the hotel its own personality, highlighted by a dominant color. Those in the lower building enjoy a variant on decors inspired by English models: floral fabrics on the walls with plant trails perched on by the occasional bird; plush fitted carpets ornamented with an eminently graphic pattern and complemented by a community of furniture from divers traditions. The upper section offers an improvisation on a 1940s style.

**Pages 56–57** In this building, Alberto Pinto provides creature comforts of the highest contemporary standards, while sacrificing nothing of the immemorial charm of its ancient stonework. In redefining the space, he planned very generous volumes for the bathrooms. Reveling in the natural color of the stone, here afforded by large flagstones on the floor and splashbacks, these open, sun-kissed rooms include a vast shower box and bathtub.

**Facing page and left** Comprising two sites, the Hostellerie de Plaisance includes a house at the top of the village and another further down connected by a subterranean transit elevator. The rooms in the upper house form a tribute to the forties spirit, individualized by a dominant color scheme that is once more echoed in randomly arranged dots on the made-to-measure wallpaper. Intent on personalizing the space to the maximum and affording fresh images of enjoyment for each new stay, the motifs appearing in the embroidery on the cushions and curtains, the fabrics, the furniture, and the engravings differ strikingly from room to room.

**Facing page** The choice of natural materials, the commitment to clean lines, the many references to the world of the Navy mean that this super-yacht lives and breathes sophisticated boating pleasure. To one side of a porthole, a bronze flambeau surmounted by a lampshade trimmed in fine leather stands out against the horizontally striped anigre veneer. Raised, the blind is finished with a strip of denim with holes edged by rivets, in what is a nod to the eyelets in sails.

**Pages 62–63** On the deck outside, a large covered saloon equivocates between interior and exterior. Handcrafted exotic wood furniture ensures passengers are comfortable and relaxed so as to appreciate the vast panorama before them. Though simple, the fabric covering the armchairs, settees, and cushions is embellished with sophisticated details. Thus all the cushions are adorned and personalized by braid and red and blue piping, in reference to the pennants of the US Navy.

# Sailing on the High Seas

In a nutshell, the name *Madsummer* means passion and heat. Its fit-out, then, is a literal translation of Alberto Pinto's usual concept of such craft, which can be summed up by the expression "On the high seas."

This 259-foot (78-meter) craft—with an interior nominated for a SuperYacht Award 2009—neatly conveys the designer's sporty and casual approach to yachting for pleasure. Its American owner stipulated an interior "cleansed" of all superfluity for sailing around the Bahamas with family or friends. And so, in spite of some imposing dimensions, the vessel—like a floating haven of leisure and relaxation—preserves a sense of intimacy and simplicity that can only enhance the flavor of a vacation.

The "couture"-inspired vision Alberto Pinto successfully transposes to the domain of interior design expresses itself here in an ability to come up with the correct "dress code" for every circumstance. An unbuttoned sportswear feel is de rigueur, and, cut in quality yet resistant materials, it blends with the luxury of made-to-measure with impressive aplomb. The emphasis is firmly placed on the quest for exclusivity: the lines of the design amount to a master class in the finest techniques, while the fluid spaces betray a consummate talent for stagecraft.

The homogeneity of the project stems from the predominant tones: the palette and other key elements derive from US Navy pennants, conjoined to a color scheme borrowed wholesale from the marine world. The materials are basic enough: leather, cotton, linen, and an unexpected hint of denim in three shades of blue stretches over the couches and armchairs in the day saloon, while exclusivity oozes from every strip of piping, every embroidered motif.

The woodwork is light in hue and the horizontally laid zebrawood seems to broaden still further the sense of horizon when the vessel is underway. Dashes of a brighter shade enliven the underlying harmony. Thus, some necessary technical equipment becomes a premise for a luminous stretch of a daring orange close to that of the starfish. On the blinds, meanwhile, rivets further reference the maritime universe, with quotations reinforced by other carefully chosen art photographs, sculptures, and prints. The six guest cabins are incorporated into this network of references, unique in both color and detailing.

The distilled core of the project and the most spectacular berth is that of the owner: with large, rectangular portholes at regular intervals, it opens 180 degrees onto the waters, giving primacy to the spectacle beyond. White and blue, the contrast between veneers in *wakapu* and plane-wood, the understated transoms on the blinds—nothing is allowed to distract from the delectable vista. For, when it comes to "total sailing," there can be no half-measures.

**Above and facing page** This easy, relaxed atmosphere reappears in the saloon on the owner's private deck. The regular stripes of the zebrawood increase the apparent volume of a room full of warmth. Chiefly a saloon in which to enjoy the daylight hours, a dynamic touch is provided by an orange block containing some necessary technical gizmos, a constraint finessed by its festive coloring. The sporty character of the *Madsummer*'s fit-out resurfaces once again in the three shades of denim that cover the armchairs, settees, and scatter cushions, all bespoke, as is the made-to-measure straw matting manufactured in Brazil. The presence of contemporary pieces ensures at once the vitality of an interior "cleansed" of all superfluity.

**Pages 66–67** In the corridor leading to the top-deck saloon and dining room stands a sculpture by Stefan Mocanu executed as recommended by Alberto Pinto. The metal structure rises from a plane-wood veneer base, the same treatment afforded the doorframes and the doors themselves. The panels are dressed with leather.

**Facing page and left** Come evening, passengers repair to the top deck and to the intercommunicating spaces of the saloon and dining room. The ample saloon is divided into islands comprising deep armchairs, couches, and footstools congregated around coffee tables. Here once more elegant simplicity is the watchword, underscored by the use of white and blue cotton. The dining-room carpet in alternate white and blue stripes is identical to that in the saloon, and echoes the predominant color scheme. Two rosewood tables, each attended by six pale sycamore armchairs of Scandinavian inspiration, are laid for dinner. Added comfort on the seats and backs is ensured by blue and white overstitched leather cushions. The standard lamps, with lampshades made of sand-treated Plexiglas, were designed by Alberto Pinto. The sycamore veneer on the walls is laid in a herringbone pattern and scattered about at random with darker wood dots, in a subtly dynamic and lively treatment of the surface.

**Left** For those moments of leisure, this guest cabin converts into a home cinema. The already comfortable ambience is made still more relaxing by the unbleached cotton panels displaying three lithographs by Miró. The shape of the settee, upholstered in unbleached cotton and accompanied by two matching cushions, is accentuated by the black lines of the saddle-stitched selvage leather straps and woven leather braid. In front of the couch, two black leather chairs are accompanied by companion footrests that can double as pull-up tables. A pair of silver-plated *guéridons*—small side tables—completes a setting devised for total comfort.

**Facing page** The warmth and scent of the covering impregnate a flight of stairs clad entirely in leather squares. Braided, the same fine, natural material sheathes the supple lines of the handrail. The steps are laid with a woven woolen carpet with the rugged appearance of straw, offering a marked contrast with the sensual smoothness of the leather. On the ceiling, the shade of the plane-wood veneer harmonizes perfectly with the general color scheme of the space.

**Right** Each cabin, with its own en suite bathroom, subscribes to a different decorative scheme, with leather the constant keynote. The color, derived from Navy pennants, thus varies from cabin to cabin, the materials being treated with a multitude of techniques: saddle-stitching for the bed-heads and banded cushions, coordinated with the bookbindings on the shelves, and twisted leather on the reading lights fitted into all the bedside tables.

**Facing page** In the cabin here, the delicacy of the braided wood veneer on the furniture joins with that of the beige cotton dressing the panels mounted on the walls. The bed-head is also cotton-covered in three differently colored pieces taken up in the fabric chosen for the cushions and the sheets, as well as in the desk chair that faces out over the sea. The en suite bathroom relies on the same simplicity, illustrated in the natural beauty shared by the oxidized travertine and the light plane-wood veneer.

**Above and facing page** With its star-shaped wall lamps this cabin next to the owner's master quarters has been specifically envisaged for a child. The matte brushed wood on the walls contrasts with the brilliant and glossy finish on the furniture, while the green and coral fabric echoed in the bed head, sheets, and blinds, affords a sprightly touch. Sporting the same brushed wood planking along the walls, the idea of unity is pursued in the bathroom that extends from the cabin.

**Left** Opened 180 degrees to the horizon, the owner's quarters lead onto a private bridge, and include a jacuzzi and a saloon. The splendid vista serves as a foil to the pared-down decor. Straw-effect woolen carpet, plane- and dark-wood veneer, leather panels over the partitions, blue and white textiles: the "casual" spirit presiding over the entire fit-out resurfaces with mastery here. This simplicity is highlighted by finesse in the detailing, such as the transoms cross-stitched on all the blinds or the suede bed-head sewn in a diamond pattern.

**Facing page** Above, the owner's cabin
extends into a small office. A space for
concentration, it marshals a full complement
of natural materials: straw-effect woolen
fitted carpet, dark-wood veneer dado,
braided plane-wood and leather paneling.
The desk, an arch of light wood pierced
by two circles on the shorter sides, has
the edges and top clad in leather. The same
circular geometry recurs in the cutouts
of the two white upholstered armchairs.
The storage unit behind the desk is
composed according to the same principle,
the sides and top of its light-wood carcass
being dressed with leather. The owner's
cabin continues with a spectacular bathroom
where natural materials are contrasted and
space is privileged to stunning effect. The
mirror, the light wood, and the dark wood
very simply picked out by a fine inlaid metal
border, a slab of blonde stone and a large
*hammam* shower built in different marbles
all convey the masculine style of this space.

**Right** The hallmark of the onboard decor
is the interplay between the materials and
the details of finish that graces the whole
interior. The checkerboard plane-wood
overlay on a door is repeated in the
composition of the marble mosaic on the
Turkish bathroom floor. These characteristic
visual correspondences bestow unity
on a project whose luxury relies solely
on expertise of the highest caliber conveyed
through noble, natural materials.

# An English Country House

Tusmore House sits in the heart of Oxfordshire, a faithful tribute to the Palladian style that developed in England from 1710 to 1760. Its plan is modeled on that of the great mansions that were created during the Hanoverian dynasty. The project in fact occupies the site of a onetime country house, long since destroyed by fire, and stands on a vast agricultural domain that glories in wide-open vistas composed of lakes, woods, meadows, fields, orchards, and gardens, all artfully disposed. A huddle of delectable cottages lies reassuringly close by. If the model is far from new, the effect remains spectacular. In the neoclassical line of the works of Andrea Palladio, Inigo Jones, and the Earl of Burlington, the house's imposing silhouette towers like a monument.

Perfectly symmetrical, it radiates out from the center as a circle inscribed within a square. The four pronaos (entrance halls) and dome are reminiscent of Mereworth Castle, or, earlier in date, of Palladio's Rotonda near Vicenza.

We are then in the century of the English Enlightenment, in the "age of connoisseurs"—that of avid collectors, of great aristocratic families who governed vast empires of trade, industry, and agriculture. We are, for the present, with one of the great and the good. Periods overlap and often merge in the palace revolution at Tusmore House, the largest such edifice to be built in England since the end of the nineteenth century.

For its interior, Alberto Pinto bases his vocabulary on the grammar of its architecture, for the classical idiom is a language of which he has total command. The objects combined here are never divorced from meaning and use; rather than coagulating into museum stagnation, the space forms a society that functions in the service of a thoroughly contemporary reality.

Moreover, the eclecticism of the period allows for a freedom of action that eschews historicity and repetition. Exhaustively documented, and in close cooperation with English Heritage, the interiors of the drawing rooms located on the first floor are not a reconstitution of the English eighteenth century, but a reincarnation. Adams, Chippendale, Gainsborough, and Turner—the sheer excellence of the period is represented by its foremost figures. Each plays their part in a civilized opulence nourished by a curiosity that has handpicked each beautiful object from the storehouse of memory and from the compass of space. The creations of a manicured Nature that unfurls before each soaring Venetian window meet those of a culture calculated to beguile the senses and feed the soul. Each room exalts its color and its spirit—ranging from the melting blue that dusts the Wedgwood cameos to a sun-kissed yellow, one after another the rooms partake of a different atmosphere, each devised to match a given hour of the day.

Yet this lengthy traveling-shot through the decorative pattern-book of the English eighteenth century allows ample space to more up-to-date concerns, the family room on pages 92–93 being a prime example. In its glorification of the pleasures of the silver screen, it recalls that Tusmore House is a waking dream, the exultant re-creation of England in an era of heroism.

**Above** Posed on the ledge of a window framed by voluminous blue silk curtains, a striking bronze seems about to step down into the scene. In the gallery, a group of engravings presents examples of classical architecture, while the walking canes in a stand beneath illustrate the infinite formal richness of these articles.

**Facing page** An upholstered leather reading chair is positioned before shelves containing finely bound books in a case whose decorative vocabulary is borrowed from that of classical architecture. The volumes spill over into a revolving bookcase, whose tiered shelves swivel about a central axle, allowing the reader easy access to any desired volume. The fluted blue drapes with darker braided borders and tassels complement the Wedgwood biscuit plaque decorating the gilded box above the valance.

**Facing page** The large drawing room boasts a collection of old master portraits and genre scenes. Surmounted by an original gilt-bronze clock, the white marble fireplace features two carved caryatids in the surround and is decorated with a floral garland beneath the mantelpiece. Like a throne before it, a low bench covered in damask speaks volumes of the skill and savoir-faire of the master upholsterers. All the nobility of their art is expressed in an interior where the atmosphere is enhanced not only by a wealth of desirable objects, but also by the intelligent deployment of textiles in every room. A black and gilded lacquer credence (Renaissance sideboard) provides a telling example of the wide range of sources from which English neoclassicism takes its cues.

**Above** The vast volume of the great drawing room dominated by a glowing green plays host to the refined elegance of the style launched by Robert Adam in the second half of the eighteenth century. The objects on show amount to an inventory of the most beautiful forms and the most elaborate techniques of the era. Even the anachronistic couches, a hostage perhaps to modern standards of comfort, have a place here, when associated with the "à la Reine" armchairs, low bookcases and large dressers on which gaze down great baroque mirrors. Ornamental antique vases converted into lamps with finely pleated shades, and porcelain ice-buckets and flower-stands punctuate a wealth of valuable objects handpicked at auction sales or on the antiques market.

**Left** This small salon hung with sun yellow fabric grandly opens out over the bucolic setting of this great estate. Three bay windows bedecked with heavy braided silk drapes are flanked by delicate two-branched sconces beneath which medals are hung. The console table against which leans a small couch bears a finely crafted gilded bronze clock and two antique-style urns mounted as lamps topped by pleated silk shades. A detail on a low bookstand evokes the work of the cabinetmaker Boulle. Note how the patina of the two busts standing on its top is identical to that of the central bronze bas-relief.

**Facing page** Beneath a characteristic coffered ceiling from which descends an elaborate drop chandelier, and facing the two full-length portraits framing the door, the heart of this drawing room is organized around a contemporary coffee table. Realized very much in the spirit and style of the time, it is attended by a small silk velvet upholstered settee and flanked by a pair of gilded bronze side tables and two armchairs covered in a leopard-print fabric that extend an elegant invitation to afternoon tea.

**Facing page and right** The main dining room offers a concentration of the pageantry and prestige of this grand estate. It can serve up to eighteen diners seated on specially commissioned royal blue velvet-covered chairs that counterpoint the hangings around the vast table in the middle laid with grace and simplicity. The old master paintings alternate full-length portraits and large still lifes. Round the edge of the room runs an immense carpet on which stand tables richly augmented with baroque carvings, together with quieter consoles in a more classical manner. An important group of Gobelins tapestries representing the twelve months of the year has been mounted into folding screens employing an original process that displays them to great advantage. And last but not least, a splendid ensemble of silverware reflects the sumptuous luxury of the evening entertainments at Tusmore.

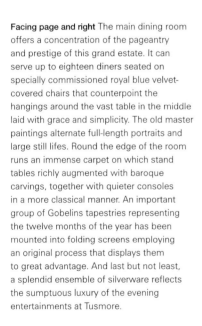

**Pages 92–93** Resolutely contemporary, the vast family room makes a leap forward in time. The columns, pilasters, and molding of the decor parallel the grandeur of the architecture, but they break totally with the era that inspired it. Opening out onto the garden and bathed in sunlight, the room is dedicated to leisure and comfort, a place where attitudes are more unbuttoned and a venue for activities such as home movies, reading, and games. Extending over a substantial area, it is organized around the home entertainment center, in front of which two large bench settees divide up the living space. White is dominant here, hit off by bright red fabric cushions and very pale yellow walls on which photographs of Hollywood legends vie with plates signed Jean Cocteau.

**Facing page and left** Although contemporary, the furniture chosen for the space refuses to sacrifice classic elegance. Though an advocate of strong contrasts, Alberto Pinto never fails to preserve unity in all the interiors under his direction. This room is a demonstrable example. Paradoxically rupture and continuity, in its contemporary style it conforms to the same symmetries and linear precision as elsewhere. Portraits of illustrious men of the past make way for the movie stars of yesteryear without the calm and ease of the Palladian era being in any way ruffled.

# The Mediterranean in a Mirror

In realizing a client's dream, it is sometimes necessary to reconcile apparent contradictions. A good example is provided by this villa clinging to the Mykonos cliffs. The owners' vision of its interior derived from two rather divergent perspectives: the husband aspired to the modesty of a "fisherman's hut," while the lady of the house had in mind something altogether more Riviera.

Alberto Pinto grasped the nettle of this paradox with brio, drawing his inspiration from the magic of the Greek islands themselves. The natural beauty of their shores, the birthplace of a thousand legends, forms an ideal setting in which to celebrate the light of the Mediterranean. Sun-kissed between sky and ocean, the villa's immaculate white form punctuates the cliff against which it huddles. The same dazzling brilliance resonates within, where it is captured and given a home.

For sir's rooms, Alberto Pinto proposed simple volumes, privileging natural materials, light fabrics, and fluid spaces. For madam, the decorator composes a symphony in curved lines, evocations of waves and rollers, reined in only by a stylized Greek meander or the crisp right angles of a staircase.

White and blue were the inevitable choice. In contrast on a cushion pattern and then on the broad expanse of a fresco that features, in reserve, heroes of Antiquity revisited in the manner of Jean Cocteau. Explicit reference to the Villa Santo Sospir in Saint-Jean-Cap-Ferrat is a constant in Alberto Pinto's artistic program for the walls of the residence. This is fulsome in the evening salon, whose color scheme evokes an abstract sunset. Pink, Parma violet, and lavender, in a jigsaw of triangles juxtaposed as if by chance, create a more feminine, powdery atmosphere. Thus daytime and nighttime clearly alternate in spaces devoted to each.

A no less relaxed attitude characterizes the house reserved for guests. Its decor distills a chill-out mood best savored barefoot and salty skinned, while its generous but homely comforts welcome visitors with open arms, fostering joie de vivre. This home riding on the waves, basking in the breeze and the gentleness of summer winds, embodies a "contemporary Greek" style. The wrought-iron banister, the spotless marble, the understated designs, a chair of intriguing shape—all speak a common language: an "aesthetic koine," in which the qualities of a place—its history, its undying culture—are expressed to realize the waking dream of a life spent in the sun's rays.

**Above** The day lounge bathes in limpid volumes awash with light. Blues and whites hail the Mediterranean daylight ensnared in textured walls, the heat tempered by the curtains and their voiles. It is a simplicity inspired by summer holidays and seaside pleasures.

The couches, designed by Alberto Pinto, are reminiscent of rocks on the seashore, but far more comfortable, the cushions set off with an embroidery pattern in a contrasting blue.

**Facing page** Down the stairwell unfurls a fresco by Dominique Derive with themes based on Antiquity and the Golden Age. In lines inspired by Cocteau and Picasso, the figures of a diver and a bather emerge from a blue background. Together with the wrought-iron banister rail and the stained glass created by Stefan Mocanu, the fresco forms part of a contemporary rereading of classical Greek culture, undertones of which resurface in the lines of a bristling conch and in a trio of marble sculptures. Curved lines and a preference for natural materials (as the wooden parquet floor and the hemp carpet braided using traditional Moroccan techniques) add to the pervasive sense of rootedness.

**Above** The architecture is totally integrated into the landscape, just as contemporary comfort goes hand in hand with the spirit of the Greek islands. On the marble surround of the swimming pool a cane daybed or a comfortable teak armchair with brick-colored cushions awaits the resting swimmer. A panama hat thrown onto a small cane table evokes feelings of sun-kissed getting-away-from-it-all and *dolce far niente*.

**Facing page** The dining room provides a stage for the encounter between the antique and the contemporary. Around the clear-cut lines of a designer glass table stand typically Greek dining chairs. Their cane bases are softened by thick cushions, that Alberto Pinto hallmark of inimitable comfort. A large white suspension lamp dissolves almost immaterially in the ensemble. The wrought-iron console and side table furnish the space to either side of a pair of sky-blue French windows. On one wall, a wooden dresser with fittings in straw continues this rustic but stylish accent that provides the keynote to the entire interior. A stone wheel exhumed during an archaeological dig stands out against the white wall with all the raw power of a piece of sculpture.

**Facing page and left** Both anteroom and
an area in which to unwind, this zone
benefits from lively geometrical frescoes
by Lenka Beillevert to create an environment
at once subdued and dreamlike. The blend
of pale lavender blue, pink, and gentle violet
together composes a space that hovers
between dawn and twilight. The cushions
on couches that extend into generous
footstools take up the color scheme in
a relaxed mood, echoed in the hand-drawn
designs on the two lampshades. The stand
of the console at the foot of the staircase
is a veritable glass sculpture, its fluid lines
answering those of the fresco and recurring
mutedly throughout the house. Supported
on a bronze stand, the glass top seems to
float in midair, while a lamp with a solid
metal foot and parchment lampshade emits
a diffuse light that flits over the shapes
and colors of the fresco. Leaning against
the wall, a geometrical composition signed
Malevich appears to reflect the interior
in miniature.

**Right** The corridor around which the various zones of the private spa are arranged is decorated with contemporary prints featuring stylized marine motifs. The glass insets in the wooden doors hint at branches of coral. This underground and secret part of the house also boasts an elaborate boudoir that amounts to a full-on beauty salon.

**Facing page** Designed for madam's exclusive use, the salon is joined by a large dressing room, a glamorous hideaway in which to prepare for a great reception. A spirit of comfort and relaxation reigns supreme in the total intimacy of a refuge conceived in the manner of a deluxe Hollywood greenroom. Beneath a chandelier stretching out its arms of coral, the sumptuous form of a unique Pelican armchair, handcrafted by the firm of Finn Juhl, stands proudly on a designer rug. The honey-colored veneer mellows the light, making it perfect for a make-up or hairstyling session.

**Above** The ocean air wafts through the guest house inspired by the simple lines of the local fisherman's huts. Once again, mythological figures on Dominique Derive's frescoes parade about a blue ground in a composition vaguely reminiscent of Jean Cocteau's decor in the Villa Santo Sospir at Saint-Jean-Cap-Ferrat, thereby linking not only two of the most beautiful shores of the Mediterranean Sea, but also two shared cultures. The white-painted coursed stone surround to the fireplace, the exposed beams, the scattered shells, the natural fiber rug gracing the floor: everything participates in a sense of unsullied naturalness, given a homely touch by the comfortable couches or the refinement of a gorgeous piece of furniture such as, for example, a small side table in bronze of a singularly exclusive design.

**Facing page** Two blue tables and their simple painted wooden chairs on the slabs of gray marble a round the swimming pool would be equally at home in a small port in the Cyclades. Beneath a pergola that abuts the classical structure of the white lime-washed house with contrasting blue shutters, another half-inside half-outside space—where curtains filter the sun and compose an oasis of relaxing shade—awaits one with some welcoming cane armchairs.

**Above** One looks through an arch built
in local stone onto a view of the terrace
and the splendid swimming pool. It is
so close to the waves that the backwash
can be heard from one of the cane chaises
longues sheltered from the sun by large
parasols. In the distance, one glimpses
another shore of the island. Nestling in such
scenery, the house appears as a timeless
port of arrival for one of the more enjoyable
episodes of the *Odyssey*.

**Facing page** The resplendent sky blue walls
in the house set aside for visiting friends
allow the space to breathe and flow
seamlessly into the sunlit world beyond.
The freshness of the simple materials and
their ornamentation is pursued in the
timbered ceiling and plain exposed beams.
A teak dining table by Jérôme Abel Seguin
on a plaited hemp rug is surrounded by
chairs covered with white linen. To the rear
stand an unusual chest of drawers and
mirror made of cane using an Italian
technique developed in the 1950s. Vintage
articles picked up with the house in mind,
they impart an original flavor characteristic of
the Alberto Pinto concept. The linen curtains
glory in handdrawn designs by the artist
Hélène Guigues-Dubois, imparting a truly
original feel.

**Right** The dominant lilac of the guest room adds to an ambience conducive at once to repose and meditation. The beating sun is forgotten in the solace offered by the colors and textures of some expertly crafted natural materials. The woolen carpet lies soft beneath bare feet, while the eye dives gratefully into the concentric circles of Dominique Derive's fresco.

**Facing page** The choice of fabrics—canvas curtains, straw-yellow cushions, silk bedspread and lampshades—centers on naturalness, as with the ocean-inspired cones of the wall lights and the organic forms of the bedside lamps. A bunch of wild flowers hinting at the pastoral world outside further enhances the festive atmosphere that emanates from this house at the water's edge. On the same table, a shell extends its graceful form and affords one final dash of poetry.

Facing page Behind the glazed front, on an absolutely white smooth floor, a thick woolen carpet, with broad curving lines, delimits a waiting area. It is partially screened off by the towering backs of two settees designed by Philippe Starck that stand face to face opposite a low table covered in leather. The result distills a space in which materials and warmth contrast with a spotlessly clean atmosphere in perfect keeping with the world of medical science.

The vast dome of a light by Ingo Maurer hangs over the seating area, imparting a sense of unity. The back wall is hung with an ornamental panel set with an iterative abstract "tablet" motif. The idiom of the entire project is couched in similar allusive terms; especially in the flow zones, where the company's chief areas of activity are illustrated by amusing icons.

# A Monumental Atrium

A company's offices are a reflection of its core identity. The nerve center of its inner workings, they are also its store window. One fine day, Alberto Pinto found himself presented with the contract to fit out the 38,000 square feet (3,500 square meters) executive offices of a brand-new pharmaceuticals concern established in Turkey, the first to have been authorized by the EU authorities to distribute its products in the euro zone. Resolutely turned towards progress and the future, the interior had to communicate an absolutely contemporary mindset, as well as the extreme rigor associated with cutting-edge medical research.

The gigantic entrance forms an unobstructed cage of light in which the interior designer can hone his vision. Around the central atrium, it is distributed over two levels, with auditorium, meeting rooms, and offices, whose doors disappear into light-colored sycamore veneer flanked externally by vertical lines in walnut.

Set with tall square columns clad in glass treated alternately in smooth and sanded bands, and drenched in daylight, the striking effect of the vast space is only increased by the dazzling composite marble on the floor. A titanic plaster fresco extends over 3,800 square feet (350 square meters) on the largest wall. Diagonal lines in a hint of cream intersect with sizable aluminum incrustations darting lithely over the entire length of the wall.

The occasional pieces of furniture also rely on disproportion. Oversize, they divide off the reception and waiting areas, constituting—together with the self-supporting staircase—the pivots around which revolves a surface that gives priority to its voids. The very curves of the staircase introduce a disconcerting weightlessness, exacerbated by the transparent glass stair-rail.

In the whole program, the horizontal flows are enhanced with pictures specially created for the project, elegant variations in scale around motifs from the world of pharmaceuticals, a decorative and playful evocation of the business that forestalls visual monotony.

Lighter hues predominate in the comfortable and functional offices, while natural and noble materials take their cue from the sober, understated office of the CEO. The furniture and carpets, produced from designs by Maison Alberto Pinto, reinstate a modernist line, while the meticulously detailed finish on the walnut (rather than sycamore) on the walls underlines the importance of the room.

Conveyed with clarity, the DNA of this energetic company is transmitted unobtrusively in a project whose cardinal virtues are transparency, rigor, inventiveness, and excellence.

**Facing page and right** Alberto Pinto manages to rein in the architectural gigantism of the immense and immaculate hall of this pharmaceutical laboratory with panache. His language underlines with sobriety the innovation inherent in medical research with delicate touches enhancing majestic volumes that reflect the economic status of a firm wholly in step with its time. In the center of the interior, the dynamically curving staircase seems to hover or fly through the space, as much furniture as function, into which the waiting areas melt. Treated as a living material, light brings out the structural rhythms of the building, coursing through the diverse textures of the glass cladding the architectural elements and technical equipment and glorying in the striking visual effects of a monumental fresco by artist Lenka Beillevert.

**Pages 116–117** The welcoming, almost homely, feel of a conference room offers a complete contrast with the brightly lit reception hall, magnitude of space yielding to comfort and concentration. The luxurious natural materials, such as the oak that not only appears on the parquet flooring but also lines the walls, create studious environment for business discussions that can take place either in a small but comfortable meeting room or in deep armchairs placed around a conference table. This all-pervasive elegance shows how the decor has more in common with a residential interior than with an anonymous office refit.

**Left** Comfortable yet conducive to reflection, the director's office shows that this is where significant decisions are taken. Treated as a private space, it boasts made-to-measure furniture in which modern inspiration and art deco blend seamlessly, as well as some works of art, poetic eye-catchers that act as spurs to thought. At one end of the room, the shape of the half-moon desk veneered in light wood hints at inspirational focus and leadership; another small room opposite offers a venue for less formal meetings. The whole benefits from a cordial atmosphere echoed in the veneer, the light chestnut-brown, thick-pile woolen carpet, as well as in the horizontal slats of the Venetian blinds filtering the sunlight.

**Facing page** Details in Alberto Pinto's design demonstrate the sheer quality of an interior put together like a haute couture gown. Peerless saddle-stitched leather enwraps a settee, delimiting the delicate edge of seat cushions upholstered in velvet chenille. The varnished wood veneer sets off the gilt bronze of the knobs designed specifically for this piece of furniture to wonderful effect. Finally, the artworks provide that personal stamp that distinguishes every project that emerges from Alberto Pinto's office. To avoid showiness, luxury has to be expressed in the perfection of every detail—the reflection of master craftsmanship and a decorative language determined by the client's personal taste.

**Facing page** A welcome in the fullest
meaning of the term is extended
by the entrance to this apartment. The ample
access corridor is like a breath of fresh air:
first, there's the art—both contemporary
and art brut—and the generous volumes.
Then comes the warm parquet flooring
that points the way to the lounge opening
out into the corridor: the ceiling-high doors
fold back into the reveal so as to disappear
completely into the wall, thereby
decompartmentalizing the space.

# Pied-à-terre in Geneva

"Youth knows what it doesn't want before it knows what it does." Jean Cocteau's quip serves as the perfect epigraph with which to introduce this apartment. The client, a young executive obliged to shuttle a great deal between London, New York, and Geneva, required a pied-à-terre in Switzerland to which he could return and immediately feel at home. But he also needed a place that would give life to his collection of paintings, somewhere he could entertain his friends or simply put his feet up. These were the only stipulations for the interior: the rest was left up to Alberto Pinto.

Was it the location in Switzerland that encouraged the designer to opt for soft-pedalled neutrality? Perhaps. The fact remains that the atmosphere, bathed in daylight that pours in from several directions, is all quietly-spoken harmony. The volumes are opened up to the maximum. For instance, once folded back, the floor-to-ceiling doors slip into the embrasure, leaving the eye free to enjoy the unobstructed view. Only natural materials are employed: grayed oak is omnipresent, warming walls, where it alternates with broad expanses of white. It encases the television set above a spacious fireplace whose stone carcass, masking the various technical components, coordinates its fluted effects with the panels surrounding it.

Limited to fine furniture, a few originally-designed rugs, and a handful of contemporary fabrics, the ornamentation presents an open invitation to unwind, a feeling seconded by the seamless tones of gray, off-white, and marron glacé chestnut selected for the various living spaces. If a bright counterpoint in red velvet or a work of art enlivens what is a masculine, unbuttoned ensemble, a convivial spirit presides over the various rooms provided with comfortable and commodious seating options. In one, facing settees invite one to stretch out and watch a movie; others serve as a venue for early evening enjoyment. All these spaces are unified by an opening that extends from the kitchenette adjoining the dining room.

The designs for the study, bedroom, dressing room and bathroom created surfaces that are more enclosed, more compartmentalized. Centered on function, they do away with superficial effects, the bespoke furniture responding uniquely to its purpose. A "tiger" rug ripples over the floor beneath the imposing desk in leather-covered wengé wood. If panels of piqué fleshside lambskin afford a subdued ambience in the bedroom, the noble stone in the bathroom drenched in daylight chimes in with the revitalizing qualities of the rituals of bodycare.

The backdrop to youthful energies channeled to good use, this apartment can look to the future with serenity. Looking down over the city, its timeless lines offer a vision of assured masculine style, complying perfectly with what any young man might desire—without his even having to put it into words.

**Facing page and above** Sobriety, the choice of natural materials and a color scheme in shades of gray and beige embody a masculine style characteristic of the lounge, which leads out onto the terrace and into the dining room. Above the flame-treated gouge-effect Jura stone fireplace, the television is set into a wall lined with brushed-wood panels housing various technical and automated components. On a large woolen rug furrowed with curves, a broad low table with Japanese-style feet offers a plain glossy black surface around which stand two deep settees furnished with cushions, a contemporary-style armchair, and some pull-up tables.

**Pages 124–125** The apartment is planned so as to open out the reception space. An extension of the lounge, the dining-room floor is characterized by a carpet's abstract design, created by the Maison Alberto Pinto. The top of the table for eight is enlivened by shallow hollows in the matt lacquer. In the evening, these attract the glow from a contemporary chandelier above, and in the day the raking light from a French window opening through to the terrace. The contemporary artwork on the wall echoes the predominant colors of the ensemble.

**Facing page and above** A second salon offers guests a coffee table sheathed in crocodile leather with two low chairs covered in foal, as well as a vast stretch of settee in red velvet scattered with a plethora of cushions in matching shades. Above them, a row of stiletto heels by the contemporary artist Allen Jones strike a sardonic note. This dynamic image diffuses its power through the environment, finding a formal echo in the original base of a small *guéridon* and the slender silhouette of the lamps.

**Left** The apartment's private quarters comprise an impressive master suite featuring a bedroom, an office, and a bathroom drenched in daylight that seems dedicated to the sky. The generously proportioned window presents a broad vista, while more light is captured in the glazed canopy above the bathtub, unconventionally placed behind a screen of mirrors above the basins and the light-wood veneer unit containing them. Metal wall cladding, in conjunction with mirror- and frosted glass, masks the shower and the lavatory.

**Facing page** Horizontal and vertical lines created by panels on the bedroom wall look through into the comforting graphic rigor of the furniture and doorframes in the office. The pale yet warm hues harmonize in the natural light, an effect enhanced by the studied association of materials.

**Left** The specially commissioned flattop desk is characterized by eminently simple lines. Wengé wood and leather mitigate a formal severity whose presence would be more than enough to furnish the room.
Large storage closets in grayed oak appoint the walls, a further demonstration of the importance of joinery in this particular contract. A carpet with a "tiger" rug motif borrowed from Nepalese iconography fosters the tactile and visual comfort of the space. A leather-upholstered metal and wood bench is a perfect fit for the geometric design of the desk before it.
A suspension lamp hanging directly over the dark leather blotter and pad delimits the writing area with precision. Set into the embrasure, the doors practically vanish to proclaim the space opening into the entrance corridor.

**Facing page and left** Lined in regular panels stretched with perforated fleshside lambskin, the bedroom proffers its invitation to absolute repose, an effect enhanced by the thick-pile carpet and a bedspread in colors that melt into the decor. Nestling in a recess fitted with a row of spotlights on the ceiling, the bed-head, conveniently appointed with two leather-whipped flexible reading lights, is flanked by two wooden bedside tables complete with a nest of three witty pull-out tables. A bench with a woven leather base stands at the foot of the bed. The interior is completed by a pair of small side tables for personal photographs and souvenirs. One stands close to the bed, while the other serves as a companion to a méridienne couch covered in garnet-red velvet. The body is absorbed by the voluptuous forms of this paragon of comfort, sinking deliciously into its thick mattress. Above it, an abstract dreamscape, all gold and grisaille, refracts the intangible vibrancy of the decor.

**Facing page** The decor of this exceptional apartment, enjoying panoramic vistas over a substantial proportion of New York, is assured not only by the furniture within but also by the skyscrapers without. Here, where the immateriality of the glass walls is counterbalanced by the warmth issuing from the materials and fabrics, the furnishings echo the architectural eclecticism of the city. Enthroned on the raster pattern of a thick wool carpet, a thirties armchair, with its modernist reading light, beckons. The corner of a settee garnished with blonde-tinged velvet sports eye-catching cushions that cry out to be touched.

**Pages 136–137** In the twilight, the accommodating interior landscape of the extensive lounge extends a shimmering welcome to the arriving guest. Divided, for comfort and conversation, into two archipelagoes composed of wide settees and armchairs set around coffee tables, the room presents an adaptable environment for evening entertaining. The immense woolen carpet woven from designs by Maison Alberto Pinto unifies the space, infused with poetry by a wealth of precious objects. Some showpiece furniture from the first half of the twentieth century plays host to eggs by Lucio Fontana and a large-format art photograph.

# View over Manhattan

How can one hope to hold one's own when faced with one of the most astounding views in all of New York? Up in the clouds, each window in this Manhattan apartment opens onto a breathtaking panorama. Perched up in the sky, this pied-à-terre belongs to one of Alberto Pinto's faithful clients, who presented him with the challenge of structuring an interior capable of reflecting the dynamism of the city outside. And, like the city, which necessarily underpins the decor, Alberto Pinto steers the composition towards a contemporary alloy of styles. Poised between Hollywood glitz and East Coast functionalism, here the designer honors an original American model.

Encased in structures of glass and steel, the apartment nonetheless breathes, expanding into the space. The soothing feel emanating from it is enhanced by the neutral setting: the composition is unified by dark-wood flooring, while the predominant tones of beige are picked up with subtly faded blues.

The centerpiece, the living room, is divided into a double suite that extends into the dining room. The various living areas are defined by vast carpets, produced after original drawings by Alberto Pinto. The designs place the accent on graphic and geometrical simplicity, some in the form of unmodulated monochromes on which congregate the generous masses of the furniture. Harking back to American fifties and sixties chic, Alberto Pinto here constructs a modernist style that revels in XXL levels of comfort, but also betrays the structural influence of Swedish design. The plaster on the walls is laid in alternate matt and gloss strips that edge into herringbone, further amplifying the volumes and setting off the "torn posters" by Mimmo Rotella dotted about the dining room. The gilded wrought-iron base of the sizable vintage table recalls ropes whipped on a ship, a hint taken up by the fringes on the carpet. Its oval glass top is echoed by the eminently contemporary suspension lamp hanging above. Around the table, the armchairs are covered in fabric with a specially designed zebra print.

Another all-important component of the brief, the master bedroom, was necessarily the object of painstaking attention. Caressed in blue, the bed, facing out over the vast panorama and with its head upholstered in satin, is flanked by wide bedside tables from designs by Alberto Pinto. Behind, a folding screen extends over the near totality of the wall. Squares left unadorned alternating with fully timbered paneling, the screen too emerged from the master decorator's inexhaustible imagination and appears to mirror the Big Apple's geometric patchwork. An important César sculpture also benefits from the generous volumes, seeming to conduct from its promontory the bustling city at its feet.

In keeping with each vibrant hour, the final factor with which the interior must deal is the shifting light, which it treats as a rhythmical conjuror, who, like a jazzman, riffs an improvisation on the theme of passing time.

**Left** The interior is encased in floor-to-ceiling glass walls, with just a few branches of broom arranged in a bouquet and reaching out above a horizon that stretches unimpeded as far as the eye can see. On the walls, a herringbone pattern in alternating matte and gloss bands of stucco shimmers as daylight falls on it. One of Mimmo Rotella's slashed movie posters tells its own story, with, in the background, part of the dining room extending the plan of the lounge.

**Facing page** Demarcated on the floor by a black woolen carpet fringed with white rope tassels, the dining room features a forties table with mounts in the shape of knotted cords and thirties chairs covered in a zebra fabric. Over the ensemble there hovers a contemporary sculptural ceiling light by Ozone. On the credence, between two elegant candlesticks, a Han horse seems to gallop through the air.

**Above** The delectably vintage tone of the
furnishings is pursued in an office arranged
in the manner of a small lounge. Entirely
lined in straw-colored braided wood,
in the light of day it revels in a gilded sheen
that continues in a carpet boasting several
shades of yellow, a color that recurs on the
cushions scattered about the white cotton-
covered couch. To the rear, near the window,
between two standard lamps with matte
gold-patinated bronze feet, a sixties Swedish
desk is joined by an armchair whose shell
is covered in weathered leather.

**Facing page** A guest room is reflected
in a looking glass clasped in a pair of slender
metal hands. As a counterpoint to the
exceptional views over Central Park,
the exclusivity of the Alberto Pinto
style—whose essence lies in achieving
a perfect blend of effects that stimulate
the senses—is wonderfully conveyed
in this association of materials and fabrics.

**Pages 142–143 and left** The blue of a sky with which this apartment is on first name terms floods over the stucco walls in the master suite. The satin bed-head and counterpane seem to have been cut out of the heavens above, as does the fabric covering the two Kim Moltzer armchairs flanking the *guéridon* table. Nearby, an important sculpture by César gazes down from its pedestal. On the other side of this imposing room, a private lounge contemplates New York as the day slips by. The floor hosts the graphic counterpoint of an abstract carpet designed by Maison Alberto Pinto and made-to-measure especially for this project.

**Facing page** The dynamic bronze body of a lamp designed by Hervé Van der Straeten twists and jives on a lofty art deco sideboard emblazoned with a rhombus pattern. Behind, a vast mirror reflects a wall decoration of black squares against a white gold ground. Once more Alberto Pinto, for whom every surface offers a space for expression, signs his intervention with a graphic flourish.

**Facing page** Passengers are welcomed onto the private jet by the understated luxury of the galley—a space dedicated to the in-flight service provided by the crew and stewards. The tone is set by the nobility of the materials, while the sober lines exude a sense of efficacy and functionality. Looking through into the main cabin, the pale tuffeau stone, the oak burr veneer varnished up to thirteen times to a perfect sheen, and the cream leather upholstery conspire to create an atmosphere at once reassuring and subdued.

# A Haute Couture Jet

While still very young, Alberto Pinto traveled a great deal. Ferried about the world by his parents and still crisscrossing it incessantly, he views the planet as a place to explore. Today this "man in a hurry," whose profession has him darting from continent to continent, knows all too well how precious time spent in transit can be. So, when a French tycoon commissioned him to fit out his private aircraft, the decorator, accustomed to this type of account, immediately understood what the requirements and needs would be. From fuselage livery to cabin interior, Alberto Pinto was offered total latitude to transform this Global Express XRS into a veritable emissary of French refinement. Fitted out as a suite, this *nec plus ultra* of the Bombardier fleet, which can fly Paris to Tokyo non-stop, carries fifteen passengers, plus crew, circumnavigating the globe without feeling like hostages to travel. In volumes combining spaciousness and discretion, each passenger can work and rest, eat and drink, and enjoy the in-flight entertainment. The project gave free rein to the Alberto Pinto concept, with hands-on, day-to-day management of the refit carried out by the manufacturer. Operating hand in glove, the uncompromising demands of the designer and the incomparable knowhow of the manufacturer have resulted in unparalleled standards of execution, in particular in terms of cabinetwork and upholstery, all underpinned by the personal touch imprinted by the art of Alberto Pinto.

Treated in a light tonal range, with the graphic accents typical of the decorator, the aircraft is fitted out in noble materials and with a high level of technical finish: silk and wool for the fitted carpet after an original design, burr oak for the partition veneers, and the furniture discreetly inset with fillets in browned brass; padded suede for the cabin, oversewn leather round the ports, seats made-to-measure, covered with off-white leather and trimmed in twisted piping and leather braid. The final outcome is a haute couture vision of aircraft interior design whose distinguishing characteristics are: luxury down to the tiniest details, contrived to flatter the eye and soothe the mind; the low-key presence of hi-tech; and an optimal interpretation of space as comfort.

**Left** The master cabin opens out initially into a square comprising four armchair recliners. Covered with cream leather, their lines are underscored by fine braid of woven brown leather strapping. Two varnished burr-oak tables rimmed with high-polish brass slide away noiselessly into the side panel veneered in the same wood that stretches the length of the fuselage, lined in white suede with diamond-patterned overstitching. This detail is in perfect keeping with the predominantly graphic idiom of the entire project. The fitted carpet designed at the Hôtel de la Victoire accentuates the depth of the cabin, while the regular geometric notes in wool or silk adhere to the chosen color scheme of off-white verging on cream and light chestnut with a smattering of black. Optimized for passenger comfort, the floor plan is calculated to afford maximum space.

**Above** The jet is fitted out to offer passengers every advantage of cutting-edge technology. Adjustability is the watchword: the armchairs not only swivel to aid conversation, they can also be tipped back flat for complete rest. Automated functionality includes lighting that can be adjusted to create the desired ambience. Immense care has also been lavished on the cabin's soundproofing and sound system. Such technical refinements are soon forgotten, though, beneath the plush finish and the panoply of thoughtful accessories: a cashmere blanket and a cushion for support demonstrate the paramount importance accorded passenger well-being.

**Facing page** All the prestige of an interior signed Alberto Pinto is exemplified in its details. The armrests sheathed in plaited brown leather, the bespoke fitted carpet, the foam-filled made-to-measure seats upholstered in padded saddle-stitched leather, the line formed by woven brown leather braid, the one-off design for a magazine rack, the satin brass inlay in the timber, the suede with its topstitch rhomboid pattern … no other agency in the world can offer standards like these that reflect the *nec plus ultra* of French decor.

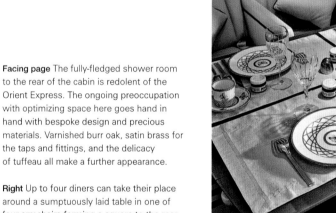

**Facing page** The fully-fledged shower room to the rear of the cabin is redolent of the Orient Express. The ongoing preoccupation with optimizing space here goes hand in hand with bespoke design and precious materials. Varnished burr oak, satin brass for the taps and fittings, and the delicacy of tuffeau all make a further appearance.

**Right** Up to four diners can take their place around a sumptuously laid table in one of four armchairs forming a square to the rear of the main cabin. Such concern with style is always at the forefront of the mind of Alberto Pinto, a designer for whom an interior can only be the result of a global approach. His office also selected the silver, glassware, and china, as well as the table settings. As befits its location, the table is laid with the "Butterfly Net" dinner service. Placed on hydraulic jacks, it can be lowered to the height of a coffee table as required. Right, the owner's tailor-made workstation. Equipped with fax, printer, photocopier, and of course a computer, wherever the aircraft may be, it can remain in business contact. The rear of the aircraft also provides space for six additional passengers in two facing settees, though the zone can be converted into a proper bedroom, the two sofas coming together to form a comfortable double bed.

# A Sense of Art Deco in Psychiko

One of the sizable residences in Psychiko—surely the most prestigious and sought-after residential district in Athens—boasts an avant-garde structure inscribed within a perfect circle. Although this vast family house has emerged from the ground only recently, its interior already seems to have garnered the rich patina of history. Composed by Alberto Pinto, it realizes the dream of a client with strong tastes, of an elaborate culture that found true intellectual complicity in that of the French decorator, who readily fulfilled the idiosyncratic remit presented to him.

The first challenge was to juggle private and public, with some spaces devoted to entertaining and others to family life. The second was to create an environment for a large collection of modern and contemporary paintings. And the third was to exalt the culture of Greece, within the context of a program presided over by the spirit of art deco. Alberto Pinto immediately saw how to make the most of the architecture. The keynote of its lines appears in the entrance hall, where the finely crafted door by sculptor Arnoldo Pomodoro introduces us to a delicate decor focused on the centerpiece of an interlace bronze table, over which hangs a chandelier whose branches extend into the space of the room. All around, ancient kraters reinforce the Greek feel. The hall leads to the heart of the residence, around which all the living spaces are distributed.

A monumental horseshoe-shaped staircase greets visitors, imparting a very special sense of majesty. Its curved risers serve the first floor containing the master suite and the second storey for the children. The gracefulness of this central elevation is underlined by swirls of wrought iron. On the floor, disks of black marble contrast with a white ground, echoing the singular form of the structure. Around this is arranged the contemporary section of the painting collection, hung in a gallery that opens onto the main drawing room and formal dining room. Such sumptuous spaces ennoble still further the materials marshaled in response to Alberto Pinto's stipulations: rosewood, mahogany, lacquered wood, silver-plated bronze, mother-of-pearl, and ivory inlay are all combined with art deco furnishings. Glorious sunlight floats over these effects and burrows into a carved plaster fresco of manifest thirties inspiration that is wonderfully set off by the parchment lining the walls. Soft furnishings too add their touch to the overall refinement in the opulent guise of crushed goffered velvet, oversewn applications, and embroidery work, as well as in delicate details such as chrome-headed tacks: lavish craftsmanship like this propels the entire design into a stratosphere of elegance. Extended into the private areas—each composed to fulfill a personal remit—this captures an ideal where modernity walks in hand in hand with references to the antique and suggests the precepts for a contemporary classicism.

**Facing page and left** Emerging from a pastille of black marble that echoes the essentially circular structure of the whole house, the monumental staircase designed by Alberto Pinto acts as the pivot around which the entire structure, with its two levels above ground floor, is articulated. The ground floor, where the family's public and private lives intersect, is composed of reception rooms distributed around a central gallery, in which hang some of the foremost masters of Impressionism and contemporary art.
To the left of a canvas by Roy Lichtenstein one looks through to the formal dining room. Framed by four enameled rosewood columns, the decor is dazzlingly finished and appointed. Around a vast mahogany table with silver-plated bronze fittings, chairs found on the English antiques' market were dressed with silver leaf and covered in overstitched green crushed velvet. The luminous beige effect on the wall, setting off a still life by Pierre Bonnard, is obtained by a process in which a light silver film is laid on then ripped off. Framed by two sconces sporting girandoles with matching candlesticks, the canvas hangs above a sideboard inlaid with mother-of-pearl and ivory.

**Pages 158–159** Ivory and royal blue join forces in the large light-filled salon. Between walls sheathed in parchment and on an immense carpet of original pattern, different areas are indicated by art deco palisander furniture and more contemporary pieces. Antique kouroi, a sculpture by Henry Moore, and Impressionist pictures punctuate a decoration afforded added grandeur by eminently haute couture details such as the motif created by the little chrome tacks driven into the bottom of the settees or the surpiqué velvet applications on the curtains.

**Right** The floors above accommodate the private spaces. On the second the children dispose of a lounge with a more "casual" atmosphere. The furniture is contemporary, while the contrast between white and blue is relayed in the thick linen covering the settees, armchairs, and cushions. Oak, wool, and leather complete a range of materials deployed with lightness and simplicity. Below is shown the first floor dedicated to the parents' suites, with a view of the office of the master of the house. Above the settee hangs a Picasso drawing, contrasting with the pale-wood panels in lightly limed oak.

**Facing page** Breakfast is served in this light-drenched blue and white room. At the height of the skirting and framing the shelving system encased along the shorter wall, a frieze of *azulejos* matches the display of blue-and-white china surrounding the flat-screen television. The blue linen-covered seats and armchairs placed around the table are further adorned with generous strips of white fabric. The forms of two plaster bracket lamps on the wall evoke the world of the sea beyond.

**Facing page and left** The cocoon-like "family room" on the parental floor is entirely lined in leather panels. The red or fawn-colored fabrics, as well as the walnut doors, reinforce what is a warm ambience. The art, from Greek antiquities to Andy Warhol lithographs, illustrate the symbiotic culture of a family at once attached to their origins and yet engaged in the contemporary world. More feminine, the mistress's office fuses traditional Chinese furniture with a bijou little *guéridon*, signed Hiquily, on a gilt-bronze foot that maintains a charming dialog with the yellow silk on a modern settee. A small framed drawing by Picasso hangs on the wall dressed with parchment.

**Pages 164–165** The master's bedroom naturally reveals a more severe and virile decor. The walls, like the cornices, are clad in panels sheathed in ivory-colored leather. The furniture is in black-enameled rosewood, while the optical contrast between the concentric black and white rectangles on the floor carpet makes the room appear still larger. The bed-head is wrapped in velvet chenille highlighted with woven leather braid. Above, a drawing by Egon Schiele imparts an erotic note to the atmosphere relayed by another drawing by the same artist that hangs above a small desk.

**Facing page and left** The crowning glory of this protean project, in which every creature comfort is appointed to perfection, the basement houses an indoor swimming pool. Its limpid waters reflect Alekos Fassianos's vast fresco, painted along an entire wall, a contemporary interpretation of an episode from the Odyssey. The sky-blue ground against which the mythological figures stand opens up the enclosed space. Opposite, on a beach of white stone, a lounge in exotic wood revels in the confusion between interior and exterior under the beady eye of a convex art mirror signed Hervé Van der Straeten.

**Facing page** A shifting vector of opulent living, the floating island that is the *Ona* is a dialog between the everyday needs of Man and his longing for the Ocean. Looking out on the infinite vista up on the outer deck, a mahogany table is simply laid for breakfast. The contrast between the lavish effect of the varnished wood and the braided straw placemats already illustrates the decorative combine chosen for the ship: simple pleasures enjoyed in a context of absolute exclusivity. To the back of the photograph, the oversize settees covered in white and ivory fabric extend an open invitation to savor the pleasures of life on the ocean waves.

# Elite Seacraft

The ocean is an unstable environment. This fact is no mean constraint when it comes to fitting out a first-class seagoing vessel where discomfort is not an option. An elite craft like a super-yacht calls for a mathematically calculated interior, with every aspect of the finish determined in advance down to the least detail.

But Alberto Pinto makes light work of these rigorous demands. It simply fortifies his vision of a completely regulated environment, crafted like the most perfect musical composition. Among so many others, the example of the 220 foot (66 meters) *Ona* is living proof of his facility at designing for life on the high seas; for a particular lifestyle is associated with watersports and sailing. Inspired by the legendary stars of transatlantic travel, he draws much from the lithe, dynamic lines of its cruise ships. This duality is wholeheartedly embraced in the *Ona*, where pleasure's only competitor is prestige. Exclusivity— as important as the rigging on a top-class yacht—was of course a *sine qua non*, together with the inevitable demands of image. For Alberto Pinto, such statutory requirements had to be addressed through design codes rooted in the immediate environment. It would be vain and of scant interest to reproduce the atmosphere of an apartment offshore, even when the volumes of such vessels are more than homely; the preference is for a hint of the beach-house style or some marine activity. The owner of the *Ona*, however, desired at least a ripple of opulence. Consequently, through an intelligent blend of quality if understated materials, Alberto Pinto and his team reconciled two complementary states of mind: on the one hand, a sustained sense of leisure that can be experienced, especially on the main deck, a hive of activity during the day; on the other, a determinedly modern edge, whose intangible luxury can be felt in the companions and walkways, as well as on the upper deck, where the influence of the great French interior designers and decorators of the thirties and forties shines through. The individualization typical of Alberto Pinto is likewise manifest in each of the four cabins. The creator's hallmark is amply expressed in the roomy master quarters, where a floor area of 1,100 square feet (100 square meters) is exceptional even for a craft in this class. The high point of the whole design, the staircase serving all four levels of the ship, is both a technical and aesthetic tour de force. Erected to Alberto Pinto's stipulations, it offers a refined meld of the most sumptuous materials—from the ivory lacquer on the guardrail to the leather cut to fit on the steps—the main thrust being provided by Macassar ebony, rendered all the more dazzling due to its contrast with gleaming chrome. Wherever the eye lights in this project embellished with a thousand details it catches sight of something truly exceptional. Tailor-made or adapted root-and-branch, the near totality of this project is unique, rigged up, and ready to sail for whatever luxurious port its elite captain sets a course.

**Left** The top bridge saloon seems clad in
pure sunlight: it streams in over walls lined
with maple, forming a ground on which
separate veneer panels impose a regular
rhythm of "X's". The design recurs on the
linen curtain material in the guise of thin
strips of raffia that intersect to form
diamonds. An ideal daytime environment,
the saloon plays host to natural materials
and textures. The braided straw armchairs
and settees are cushioned in simple white
cotton with lavish applications of blue- and
coral-stained defleeced lambskin, with
matching scatter cushions. The heart of the
decor is occupied by a table in sycamore
designed by Maison Alberto Pinto that
reveals a taste for the unexpected that is
here adjoined to a flair for functionality.
Ingeniously, whereas the drawers conceal
a raft of technical components, the trays
in the top can be removed for service,
revealing a coral lacquer inset on the
back that can be deployed as required
as a table setting.

**Right** The evening saloon next to the main deck is characterized by a steady pulse. On its striped woolen fitted carpet are a Macassar ebony table with chrome ornamentation designed by Maison Alberto Pinto and twin facing couches. The dining room on the upper deck—a detail of which is visible here—opens into the saloon. On the linen-fitted carpet, the two bespoke tables can be joined by means of a removable extension. They bear chrome fittings and coral and blue leather inserts. Externally the chairs are wrapped in straw edged in leather held by chrome tacks; inside they are lined with leather.

**Facing page** The hall is reminiscent of the prestige of the art deco style and the codes of classic yachting that climb the Macassar ebony-veneered staircase with its chromium-plated metal railings, its treads sheathed in cut-to-measure ivory leather, and its maple banister. In the corridors, the walls are lined alternately with panels of plaited straw and squares of leather, the contrast enhanced by the vertical veining of the wood. Chrome doorhandles covered in topstitched leather and the leather lacing sewn into the sycamore proclaim the excellence of traditional craftsmanship and elicit a unique emotional response.

**Left** The dining room on the main deck
extends into a saloon. Two spaces are
partitioned with dividers that can be kept
closed and then slid open to delight guests
with an opulently laid table. It must be
conceded that it is impressive enough when
empty. It took six months of technically and
aesthetically demanding metalworking and
cabinetmaking by the Degroote and Mussy
company to turn the design into reality.
The three specially designed ceiling lights
were treated with white-gold leaf. The chairs
reproduce a thirties model enhanced here
with a covering in period cotton re-
embroidered with moss-stitch in a dots
and diamonds pattern. The walls are
veneered in pale sycamore partitioned
by bands in Macassar ebony studded
with guilloche chrome quadrates that
recall—pursuing the allusions to the world
of the luxury liner—their oversize bolts
and rivets.

**Left** Personalized in the same spirit as the cabins, the en suite bathrooms offer an island of freshness and simplicity. Smooth cerused oak, in a gadroon effect on the cornices; imperador marble; carved and brilliant-varnished sucupira wood, associated with white perlatino marble: a vast array of materials and contrasts has been marshaled to conjure up this urbane atmosphere.

**Facing page** Inspired by flags and pennants, in this room the decoration concentrates on three plain fabrics combined in asymmetric geometric patterns or else in designs resembling an ensign. On the walls, the cerused oak veneer is animated by thumb-molding effects that act as a foil to the plain smooth paneling. In the second cabin, the keynote motif is the branch of coral. Embroidered in a large format on the bedspread, it recurs on the blinds in asymmetric branches; the motif continues in two sizes on the handles and in the form of the bronze bracket lamps painted in the predominant hue and topped by made-to-measure lampshades with mother-of-pearl buttons and edged with coral soutache.

**Right** The expansive master cabin amounts
to a fully-fledged apartment nestling in the
heart of the yacht. When the partition
separating them is opened, the twin rooms
seem to reflect one another in an invisible
mirror. The clean-cut lines of the decor are
enlivened with discreet couture flourishes,
such as the leather cording sewn in a broad
saddle-stitch on the anigre veneer and the
cornices, the applications of black leather
bands on the bed head, and the geometric
embroidery on the chenille cushions.
The heavy cabling round the corners of the
bedframe in anigre again alludes to the
world of the Navy. The thirties-inspired
bedside tables are characterized by
a contrast between black leather and beige-
colored velvet calf. The adjoining saloon
explores similar graphic effects,
underscored by black filleting between the
boards of the parquet floor. The artwork on
the wall is once again signed Marco Del Rey.
Surmounted by lampshades accented by
sewn black leather, the lamps with stems
composed of a column of chromium balls
were acquired on the antiques market.

**Facing page** Madam's dressing room
plunges us into a more feminine universe.
The Cosmati mosaic work of cut Murano
mirror-glass, the whitened zenobia, and the
sycamore parquet flooring create a subdued
atmosphere enhanced by the satin blinds.
With a companion chair dating from the
forties, the coiffeuse (dressing table with
mirrors) was designed by Alberto Pinto
and is surmounted by two opalescent
green lamps.

**Left** At times, passengers gather in the home movie theater to lounge on its comfortable sofa beds and deep armchairs. Their rough cotton covers are perfectly coordinated with the tone of the anigre parquet flooring. The same wood on the wall is striated with black wooden bands forming behind the screen a visual effect redolent of a reel of film. A detail in the master dressing room shows the importance given to bespoke finish, as in these drawer handles sheathed in leather or else composed of a simple assembly of saddle-stitched cordons. The perlatino marble in this small restroom is inlaid with squares in Macassar ebony.

**Facing page** The individual touch of the black leather details resembling belt loops on the armchair cushions resurfaces on the blinds. Specially conceived by Alberto Pinto, the armrests are fitted with convenient trays-cum-reading lights. Lastly, this paean to comfort is completed by a white cashmere stole thrown over the back of each seat.

# Indian Summer on the East Coast

The current owners fell for this vacation residence because of its great trees. Time-worn and majestic, survivors of countless storms, they soar with dignity in a park on a level with the water, benefiting from grandstand views in the vibrant Indian summer.

The main range of buildings nestling in the heart of all this nature has been remodeled to cater for a philanthropic family on their weekend breaks in the fall. Nearby, a guest house, a poolhouse with a half-inside half-outside sports complex, a teahouse, and a fisherman's cottage form a microcosm dedicated to the wellbeing and delight of their visitors. Demanding nothing but the best, the team assembled included Belgian landscape designer Jacques Wirtz, the architecture firm Roger Ferris & Partners, and finally Alberto Pinto, who was appointed to oversee the project.

The interior designer was presented with carte blanche over the entire decoration agenda. The only items bequeathed by the client were a pair of clothes-stands by Jacques Adnet, and they now play their role in creating a feeling of coziness that embraces visitors in the last lingering days of the season.

An elegance stemming from a subtle balance between modernity and tradition, characteristic of the work of both architect and decorator, the refinement of oversewn leather sheathing, has inspired an informed and original eclecticism rooted in modernity. In consequence, Alberto Pinto composes his tableaux with artistic objects rather than with utilitarian forms, exploiting the delicious textures of natural materials, in a vibrant and colorful art. Alberto Pinto's remarkable planning abilities constitute one of the foundations of his craft. As in each and every composition, he immediately realized how best to translate the volumes here into a potential for function or decoration. Filling an imaginary portfolio with a vast range of materials, fabrics, artworks, furniture, *objets d'art*, and right down to the china and household linen, before he can provide it with the richness of a complex and individual soul and identity, Alberto Pinto has first to imagine himself living in the house. The note of exclusivity here can be gauged by the prestigious names whose talents combine in the ornamentation, the unseen narrative holding them together being underwritten by Alberto Pinto.

If each space in this family house possesses an atmosphere of its own, the artworks in each room vibrate in unison with that atmosphere. Paradoxically, its very homogeneity arises from juxtapositions born of elective affinities, rather than from the collecting impulse. Alberto Pinto's creations act as links in the chain that encircles the overarching harmony of the project and provides the finishing touch to a design whose outlines could scarcely be imagined from the empty space. Each fresh discovery encountered in room after room cultivates feelings of both intimacy and grandeur.

Here, the artworks fulfill much the same role as the massive trees in the park: leitmotifs around which the flows and perspectives are arranged. And, like that of the garden, the success of the interior lies in the sense of reassuring familiarity it conveys.

**Facing page and left** A pair of nineteenth-century Anglo-Indian armchairs repose on the carpet, designed by Maison Alberto Pinto; the side tables next to them are seventies examples by Philippe Hiquily. The eclectic allure of this interior is exemplified by the four fifties flower-stands by Christofle on the American coffee table, the plates from the same period signed Picasso, and the overstitched leather standard lamp by Royère. The entrance hall provides a chance to admire the floor throughout the house, a patinated two-tone white-painted calpinage on oak. The bright colors of a forties tapestry by Marc du Plantier stand out on terracotta-striped white walls. This in turn is framed by a pair of armchairs covered in untreated silk by Kim Moltzer, across from which rises the sweeping lines of the banister and balusters of a staircase designed by Alberto Pinto. Beneath it, a Lalanne torso stands on a table in Flemish baroque style. The credences are signed André Sornay.

**Pages 186–187** The breakfast room opening onto the magnificent scenery extends a small lounge boasting a large settee covered in coral-colored linen with patterns by Alberto Pinto. The same energetic color scheme recurs in the pattern on the carpet, inspired by a *suzani*—a Central Asian textile. Before the couch an Ado Chale seventies bronze coffee table is adorned by japanned work from the late nineteenth century. The chandelier hanging above the table is by Claude Lalanne.

**Right** On the walls of the dining room, which is furnished with twin tables, charcoal sketches drawn by Madeleine Massonneau in the thirties—for a since vanished fresco that once decorated Saint-Nazaire city hall—are hung. To the rear, on two false marble columns, stands a pair of photophore lamps signed Poillerat. In the foreground of this view of the great salon, facing the settee wrapped in contrasting damask one finds a pair of twenties armchairs from the Yves Saint Laurent collection. In front of them shimmers a forties coffee table, a *guéridon* by André Sornay, and, further back, a pair of forties lamps by James Mont in ceramic gilded in gold leaf.

**Facing page** A fifties American table with white enameled base and black varnished top enters into total complicity with the Empire silhouette of the early nineteenth-century Russian chairs, whose black varnish is inlaid with a palmette motif in brass. The color of the seats in pearl-gray embroidered silk is perfectly coordinated to the rugged effect of hand-tufted linen carpet. The original plaster ceiling light is shaped like a decorative clamshell hung with coral and dark bronze baubles. The doors and cornices are in white-patinated brushed oak.

**Left** The grand lounge opens completely onto the veranda and its view across the shore. This decompartmentalized reception space can thus readily be modified to match the number of visitors. Pushed up against the couches, the low furniture was created after original designs by Maison Alberto Pinto. The large linen carpet extends to a silver jardinière. Between interior and exterior, the veranda displays two fifties armchairs by Jansen, a child's bench by Claude Lalanne, and two large fifties American side chairs covered with a printed fabric.

**Facing page** To one side of the couch an early twentieth-century Viennese table has landed. The large jardinière, with its double basin in staff, designed by Maison Alberto Pinto plays host to a liberal spread of fern. The bright color of the prints contrasts with the black sisal carpet, whose somber intensity reinforces the luminous opulence of a space that dialogs with the spectacle of nature outside.

**Right** Beneath a structured ceiling, the pearl-gray, white, and blue color scheme in the bedroom belonging to the mistress of the house exudes a subdued and urbane atmosphere that is a reminder of the allure of the art deco style. The effect is encouraged by the works of some of its foremost masters, such as an eggshell-encrusted Marcel Coard commode of the twenties, a comfortable armchair by Paul Dupré-Lafon, a small footrest by Jean Royère, and an ebony stool by Paul Iribe join forces on a large Chinese silk carpet dating from the beginning of the twentieth century. A small thirties console table with a looking glass, a silver-plated bronze bench acquired on the antiques market, and a fifties plaster mirror flanked by two Lalique wall lights complete this inspirational picture gracing a fabric wall decoration.

**Facing page** In the television room adjacent to the main suite: two méridienne couches present a mix of cotton, leather, and cashmere after a design by Alberto Pinto. The walnut parquetry walls are lined with a raw cotton fabric ornamented with doweling. A thirties Moroccan carpet enhances the sense of comfort. The walls in madam's bathroom are entirely lined with straw marquetry, associated with silver-leafed guilloche work. The storage units are masked behind paneling. The carved wood looking glass, made after drawings by Alberto Pinto, stretches majestically above the Italian stone countertop. The straw-covered chair in front of the small dressing table is a masterpiece of the thirties by Dominique.

**Facing page and left** The guest rooms are all characterized by attractive originality. Hung with lemon-yellow woolen wall covering, the first is all curved lines. Red metal circles support the tapering feet of a Hubert Gall console table surmounted by a round red-lacquer mirror of the American seventies. The torsion effect displayed by the stool in staff by the Michael Taylor resurfaces in the spirals on the woolen carpet designed by Alberto Pinto, who also signed the household linen and the two T-frame bedside tables. The bench at the foot of the bed is a Danish creation of the sixties. Elsewhere, the eyes in a carpet by Paco Rabanne gaze up at a ceiling that imposes its architectural language on the bedroom. White verticals adorn the gray walls at intervals, in an unobtrusive neutral tone awakened by the thick embroidery ribbon that girdles the bed head. Its apple-green hue is repeated on the foot of the bed and on the printed curtains, whereas the graphic effect of black-and-white makes a further appearance on the fifties English bedside tables and the black perforated-steel bench by Xavier Lust. In one bathroom, the neutrality of creamy textures harmonizing with the rich tonality of the Italian stone is given an added twist by oxidized metal fillets inset into the white lacquer of furniture, a gold and silver mosaic rug, and by the high-impact relief on the walls.

**Pages 196–197** Between two greenhouses growing orchids, the pavilion in the garden is conceived of as a lounge that opens on the outside through vast bay windows of moresque inspiration. Allegories of the seasons in the form of two eighteenth-century Italian sculptures frame an upholstered sofa covered in white straw. The wrought-iron and travertine coffee table in front of it is signed Royère. The floor in blue travertine sets off the verdigris bronze foliage plant made by the American artist Kent Bloomer.

**Right** The home entertainment room is wainscoted entirely in "candy-striped" natural wood, whose colors inspire the choice of fabrics on the easy chairs and settees placed on the Brazilian straw matting. This warm atmosphere is furnished by two long Chinese low tables from the beginning of the twentieth century, a settee in walnut topped by a bronze lamp, and a *guéridon* by Hervé Van der Straeten whose base performs a veritable ballet in bronze. This is in turn surmounted by a lamp converted from a pharmacist's glass globe, its body echoing the form of the contemporary convex mirrors with their intricate papier-mâché frames. In front of the fireplace, the striking note from a bench with a linear motif embroidered on a midnight-blue ground brightens up the color scheme of the room.

**Facing page** The relaxed "Pop" poolhouse saloon is a place of brio and zip. A picture by Roy Lichtenstein, seventies armchairs covered with bright yellow fabric, a white resin side table, a collection of Danish vases in multicolored glass produced by Otto Brauer in the sixties—this zestful decor explodes into life against a backdrop formed of black and white walls in brushed oak, and enameled lava flooring tiles made by Ulrike Weiss after motifs created by Alberto Pinto.

# Business Duo in Athens

Female. Male. This old duality is readily accepted in reference to the private sphere. In a home, each member of the couple requires their own space as the expression of their identity. The result is the idea of a suite for "Her" and another for "Him".

Such arrangements, though, are less common in a work context, but they were paramount in the present project—indeed this was its key characteristic. The clients, a Greek couple, wanted to install both their Athens offices in one and the same construction. Both work out of one floor of a building erected for the 2004 Olympic Games, an example of contemporary architecture with generous curves redolent of a thirties steamboat.

The neutral zone of the reception hall testifies to the considerable cachet of its slimmed-down modernity. At its heart, the gracious curves of the spiral staircase snake like a white ribbon through the space. Its clear glass guardrail underscores the dimensions of the architectural plans signed by Alberto Pinto. In its well, a buoyant glass wire sculpture by Anna Skibska forms the foot of an intangible column that vanishes into the zenithal light. The contrasts start here: between curve and horizontal, between the dark Macassar ebony and light walls enlivened along the corridors and circulation spaces by geometric abstract fresco reliefs. And finally there is that between expanses of dark-wood parquet flooring and stretches of fitted carpet: technical as well as aesthetic, this last alternation moreover allows complete control over the room's acoustics.

Using this bipartite division, Alberto Pinto visually defines a sense of rigor, combining it with fluidity that interconnects the floors, and distinguishes—without opposing—madam's professional space from sir's. The treatment of the couple's respective offices exploits the potential of generic features, without falling back on cliché: it is a perilous exercise, here carried off with sensitivity.

On the feminine side, sophistication and refinement: in an idiom that derives from the designer furniture, the tonalities are those of gold leaf, grayed shagreen, light-hued sycamore; the materials, ivory or gloss crackled lacquer, parchment, oversewn leather, Macassar ebony. For madam, each space is delineated by a decorative schema dictated by the keynotes of finesse and assurance.

On the master floor, emphasis is placed on efficiency and simplicity: in aristocratic fashion, the materials, light and dark oak, take a back seat, while the furniture takes the stage—for instance, the cerused black-patina wood desk surmounted by what looks like a bronze plaque microrelief etched with the silhouettes of Athens and Piraeus.

The sum total of these contrasts emerges—the unique hallmark of the creator Alberto Pinto—in the twofold harmony that suffuses the environments of serenity and of power.

**Facing page and right** Comfort and
refinement in the conference room are
instilled by the large made-to-measure work
table in dark oak wood. The bronze plate
fixed into its top is a relief showing the port
of Athens, a visual allusion to the business
activities of this company, headed by a major
Greek shipping magnate. The carpet on the
floor is also original, woven from a drawing
executed for the project. The light oak lining
the walls was carefully judged to
counterpoise the dark oak of the desk, while
under the windows additional rhythm is
supplied by a lighting system fitted into
the woodwork. The reception space exploits
contrasts between materials and textures
to provide a contemporary coherence.
The modulation of parquet flooring and fitted
carpet is, though, not merely aesthetic,
as it is also instrumental in noise reduction.
Alberto Pinto took the necessity of
reconciling a significant number of technical
constraints in the interior architecture
in his stride. As a supplier of custom-made
solutions, he has over the years acquired
an entire network of top French craftsmen.
Here, for instance, the staircase complete
with its glass rail was made in Brittany, while
the walls display stucco fresco work by
Lenka Beillevert.

**Pages 204–205** Madam's office is naturally
of a more markedly feminine resonance.
On the black oak parquet floor, each piece
of furniture shimmers like a jewel: like this
low round table from Brazil. The couches
and seats arranged around it are covered
in silk. The panels of parchment on the walls
are studded horizontally with leather
crosspieces; the walls open into niches
framed in gold leaf.

**Right** For Alberto Pinto, luxury is defined by an accumulation of details that should reveal themselves only gradually. This is illustrated, for instance, in the juxtaposition of Macassar ebony and chrome-plated metal netting, as well as in the leather fittings underlining the horizontal strips of parchment extending over the wall, or by the treatment of the veneers. Originally designed furniture and carpets enhance an environment that fulfills the clients' desires to the full.

**Facing page** In the gentleman's domain, the rooms are decorated more neutrally, but no less elegantly. Blackened and silvered oak veneer embellishes the woodwork. The deep couches and armchairs are covered in velvet chenille. Here again, the carpet was specially designed and the furniture handpicked with the project in mind. The two wire mesh lamps on the side tables flank a settee with a welcoming configuration. The bathroom is decorated in the same vein and would be worthy of one of the world's finest international hotels.

**Facing page** An ideal venue for entertaining
guests, this apartment in the heart of London
redefines contemporary chic in terms of
black and white. Beneath a large chrome
chandelier, a special commission from
the designers Ozone, one of the dining-room
tables is surrounded by black chairs covered
in white cotton with lozenge-shaped dots.
Two intriguing copper polygonal balls
seem to float in front of the thick wool
and hemp curtains.

# In Black and White in London Town

This surprisingly spacious apartment occupies a disused library in the heart of the British
capital. Distributed over four levels, it provides Alberto Pinto with a canvas on which
to create an exercise in space. Far from being overwhelmed, he treats its imposing proportions as a springboard, an inspiration, reveling in the freedom they offer.

The customer is one of the interior designer's regular clients. Usually relatively classical in his tastes, he was won over by Alberto Pinto's instinctive preference for a
contemporary treatment, close in spirit to that of a loft apartment. The immensely elegant
result lends itself with equal grace to daily life as to entertaining. Sparseness and fluidity
are the keynotes for a couple whose lifestyle is that of urban connoisseurs, who enjoy the
presence of select artworks and designer furniture, as much as the company of their
friends for gastronomic extravaganzas.

Black and white forms the underlying contrast, the modern chic duality par excellence,
which allows for a vast array of coordinated textures, the entire space (save for the bathrooms) unified by dark-colored parquet flooring. In a similar shade, the impressively ample
doors partake of the immense sense of space imparted by the 20-foot (6-meters) ceilings.
Calculated to disappear completely when open, they leave the space unencumbered and
allow the volume to be modified at will. The doorframes structure the view, releasing the
lines of a plan adaptable to every conceivable circumstance.

Throughout the project, the walls were dealt with in a truly exceptional fashion: the
plaster fresco was worked into scratched and pinked effects that capture the light in diag-
onals, or circles of differing depths, set off in several places by yellow or white gold leaf.

The effect magnificently reinforces the spectacular well of a self-supporting staircase,
a veritable architectural tour de force: its revolutions were the subject of painstaking preparation, while the significant stresses and strains on the glass balustrade presented a
considerable technical challenge. Stucco is not the only technique deployed in revitalizing
the vertical surfaces: in the generously proportioned living room that opens into a kitchen
designed for cuisine of the highest order, they are divided into horizontal strata that allow
the space to breathe. It was this determination to eschew any hint of monotony that led to
the spectacular veneers on the cabinetwork and to the creation of wall gardens that are
reflected in the myriad mirrors in the guest restrooms.

The exceptional character of this voluminous apartment does not stem merely from
the price of a square foot in London; more tellingly, it originates in a brilliant appreciation
of the quality of its space and of how best to exploit it. Flexibly apportioned around the
demands of its occupiers, open to the world, yet comfortable, it adapts with grace to the
requirements of the moment.

**Left** The dining room is accessed through a corridor fitted with a glass-doored wine cellar. Black parquet floor unifies the space in the loft spirit that characterizes the entire interior. Hollows in the black-varnished wood floor-to-ceiling doors shimmer in the light. The doors open into the dining room, which itself leads straight through to the kitchen, where a pair of round tables mean the atmosphere remains convivial even with a large number of guests.

**Facing page** Above the kitchenette, where some of the world's foremost chefs perform feats of culinary excellence for the hosts, a series of differently designed suspension lamps illuminates the black enameled lava work-surface. A broad spectrum of the most sophisticated induction-cooking components fills the open-plan kitchen. As the technical elements are entirely concealed, visual continuity between the reception and preparation spaces is ensured.

**Pages 212–213** Drawing room, dining room, and kitchen follow one another in a single spatial plan. A torn poster by Mimmo Rotella hangs on the stucco wall, which presents three broad horizontal bands in modulated gray. An elegant correspondence arises between the padding on the generous couch and the honeycomb effect on the door panels and jambs.

**Facing page and right** On a foal carpet composed of several pelts, a couch designed by Philippe Starck and armchairs created by Alberto Pinto (and now issued in the Rio collection) dialog around a coffee table sporting an etched, gilded, and acid-treated glass top. The fireback is also made out of etched glass realized by Bernard Pictet in accordance with the recommendations of Alberto Pinto.

**Left** The space, caressed by the mysterious light emanating from the backlit rock crystal plaques forming the basin in this powder room, is a true anthology of material effects. Hollowed wood, stucco in gray and black bands, and a large mirror with a metalized wood frame create a surprisingly lively atmosphere. The tropical jungle universe into which visitors are plunged upon entering another powder room at the entrance is no less phantasmagoric. The plant-draped walls are reflected ad infinitum in the mirrors, making for a luxuriant environment in counterpose to the gleaming minimalist cylinder of the white basin. The frosted glass door separating the space from the entrance to the apartment channels the daylight into a vestibule decorated entirely in stucco fresco by Lenka Beillevert. Stage-managed by "director" Alberto Pinto, relief effects and sunbursts in yellow or white gold leaf by the artist mark the flow spaces.

**Facing page** With a square footprint scarcely thirteen feet (four meters) down the side, the veritable technical tour de force of the staircase imposes its presence from a self-supporting structure of dazzling buoyancy. The glass balustrade underscored by a fine white guardrail allows one to appreciate kinetic effects relayed by the relief in the stucco. With deep furrows or shallow pits, the striking plastic modulation of the walls fractures the light and casts intriguing shadows.

**Pages 218–219** An architectural witticism dreamt up by Alberto Pinto, the hearth of an ethanol fireplace traverses the wall, dividing the double lounge and framing a gigantic couch surmounted by a drawing by Christo. The picture is completed by a "flaque" table especially created for this interior standing on an understated woolen carpet. The latter table is composed of a tubular bronze foot and a gallery encasing a pale-wood parquetry top. The ensemble highlights the contrast between the bush-hammer surfacing on the rusticated Burgundy stone and the finely scored wall at the rear.

**Facing page and right** The large living room divided by an elliptical wall is composed of furniture consisting of one-off creations and a selection from the finest designer catalogs. The back wall displays a triptych of three outlines of the coast of Africa in glass mosaic and white coral. Two bears in gilded metal stand good-natured guard to the entrance to the study. A *Marilyn* by Mimmo Rotella adds color to the wall. The fresco, muted when serving as a backdrop to artworks, is all grace and abandon when set free on the walls. It comes into its own on an empty stretch opposite a small dining room that extends the wide open spaces of the large lounge, anticipating the effects pursued in the sideboard doors.

**Left** A haven of black light, the master dressing room is a surprising creation that has no truck with conventional codes. All in non-colors, it fosters a timeless, nest-like environment, exploiting the graphic effect of the squares on the wall hangings and the cupboard doors. The latter are reflected in mirrors, providing an illusion of perfect symmetry. This space extends through to a bathroom characterized by a halo of white light running round the undulating shape of the stucco mirror (bottom, right). On the black granite flooring, the white enamel basin unit features chrome fillets that inscribe right angles and squares around a round opener. The contrast is absolute in madam's bathroom, whose walls are lined in onyx and where the oval white bathtub hugs the contours of an alcove with a patinated bronze effect.

**Facing page** Different again, the master bedroom is a clean-lined white cocoon with walls of stucco. Pearl-gray cushions lie scattered about the enveloping form of the bed head. The sheathed leather bedside tables are bespoke, while the substantial carpet was woven based on drawings by Alberto Pinto. A braided leather bench at the foot of the bed, together with the voluptuous contours of the seating, adds to the prevailing sense of comfort.

**Above** The entrance to the private part of the apartment is made through a corridor whose wall contains a bar enlivened by wood veneer visualized as a extension of the fresco that runs through other zones of the residence. The use of oak, blackened and rubbed in circles then enclosed by gilded copper fillets, conveys a feeling of warmth and intimacy.

**Facing page** In the television room, all the technical paraphernalia of the home cinema is ensconced behind the elegant wood paneling extending above the substantial fireplace. It also masks wall cupboards, with relief handles forming an integral part of the design concept. The rug was woven after an original one-off design in coordinated colors. A dual-purpose footrest and coffee table, the upholstered bench accentuates the sensation of comfort fostered by embroidered cushions, easy chairs, and a settee, at the end of which a side table presents the geometric motifs of circle and square.

# A Refuge in La Palmeraie

There are places on Earth which put one in mind of Paradise. This property, nestling in the palm plantation in Marrakech, is one of them. Like Eden, it is first and foremost a garden, the remains of the venerable green lungs of the Red City, gradually gnawed away by luxury tourism.

Built in 1920 in the European taste, the farm renovated and enlarged by architect Gae Aulenti (assisted by Studio KO) is the embodiment of the changing face of these grand colonial houses on vast estates that offer a glimpse of the history of generations of well-heeled expatriates.

A stretch of land planted with glorious palm and olive trees, bougainvilleas, and rose bushes surrounds this residence where Tolstoy's son once came to have a rest cure. Today the property of a key figure in the world of elegance, the house is a celebration of the encounter between the artless generosity of the Orient and the artful lifestyles of the West.

Who other than Alberto Pinto could hope to forge such a synthesis? The Moroccan sun shines on his childhood memories, embroidered by the colors of an imagination since led by insatiable curiosity. With this project, the decorator attains the acme of lightness.

To fulfill the requirements of the lady of the house, the interior tallies with the cultivated simplicity of the garden. Never raising its voice above a whisper, Pinto's design is based on an oscillation between inside and out. A fusion of unsophisticated materials sophisticatedly worked, with an undertone of traditional techniques, the ornamentation embeds—without imprisoning—the estate in the culture of the home country. The soberly eclectic range of furniture and objects was handpicked to accompany a *dolce vita* that shuns ostentation. Simple cane chairs stand by an antique Syrian side table, in an admixture that usually only the passage of time can create.

One of Alberto Pinto's consummate talents is knowing how to melt into the background and let a site speak for itself. Here, in a place seemingly unaltered since wealthy Europeans would overwinter in Marrakech, he has distilled the quintessence of ease and homeliness.

The sun-drenched, gentle climate enters each and every room, as if they were open to the world outside. Here, *zellige* mosaic tiles mimic the trellis in a winter garden, while an openwork *meshrebiya* entraps the sun's rays, scattering them over the floor, as if through a palm-frond. Everywhere hovers the tranquility, the contentment of a Matisse, the touching spectacle of a golden age spent in an Arcadian realm, a refuge untroubled by the vicissitudes of history.

Into this harmonious tangle of history, Alberto Pinto weaves sobriety and restraint, in what is an Orientalist vision cleansed of all stereotype. A past master in the art, he calculates his effects to perfection, adding hints of modernity to create, like a botanist crossing wild roses, a truly unique bloom, the queen of the garden.

Pages 228–229 Simplicity and freshness are features of a large lounge where natural simplicity rubs shoulders with sophistication. As the thick walls limewashed with *tadelakt* plaster and the great cerused beams reveal, this room preserves the original structure of a farmhouse that has been enlarged several times. Alberto Pinto's aim was to enhance its considerable charm by blending the North with the South. The embroidery, generous rugs, side tables, and curiosities are all of local origin, but the white linen-covered cane furniture, the armchairs, and the settees are in the European taste, as is the rare collection of etchings featuring birds and this majestic canvas by a Spanish master.

Facing page and right Around the fireplace, the salon conveys an exotic spirit also tangible in the linen and cane furniture. Orangey yellow Moroccan embroidery on the cushions gives zest to an otherwise relatively plain fabric. A pile of citrus fruits arranged in a basket, a scattering of fresh rose blooms, an armful of sunflowers offer bright notes that translate to a love of long walks and the rapt contemplation of the passing seasons. And the veranda along the main front serves as the ideal observatory. Opening onto the lounge, it is one of many transitional spaces between inside and out. Large mosque lanterns adorn an exposed beam ceiling ornamented with geometric *tataoui* in the purest Berber tradition. Under this timbered sky, domestic comforts are extended by the woven cane settees and armchairs and by coir floor matting.

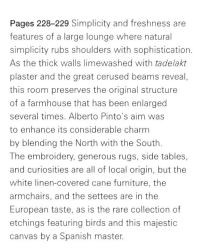

**Pages 232–233** The junction between
the original core of the house and
the contemporary section is marked by
a venerable double-leaf door in carved cedar.
Studded with copper furniture, it was rehung
during the complete refit orchestrated by
Alberto Pinto. Visitors are greeted by an
English portrait of Lawrence of Arabia on an
easel. The wall is adorned with a motif that
reworks an original local technique called
*gebs*, emulated here by sanding wood and
applying whitening through a stencil.

**Facing page and left** The welcoming and
heart-warming winter lounge is ensconced
beneath a painstakingly restored ceiling
in thuja. The walls are painted with stencils
in traditional motifs, while straw matting
muffles the floor. The cane armchairs and
settees are either provided with thick printed
cotton cushions, or padded and upholstered
in white cotton. A predominantly bright blue
collection of views of Naples punctuates
the walls. A door open to the terrace reveals
a wrought-iron table in front of a carved
wood parapet. In the fireplace, the finesse
and smoothness of *tadelakt* is married
to the cut-tile *zellige* mosaic running around
the hearth. Above the mantelpiece hangs
a richly worked silver and copper mirror.
Glazed ceramic fruits are arranged on small
mother-of-pearl and ivory inlay tables
of Syrian origin.

**Facing page** Beneath a lantern of blown glass, in the cool *menzeh*—a kind of traditional bow window protected from the sun by a wooden *meshrebiya*—stretches a bench covered with Fez-stitch embroidered cushions whose thread echoes the prevailing almond green of the decor. In front of the divan, an old carpet shows off two small Syrian side tables. The striking effect on the walls is the result of green and white *zelliges* arranged into trompe-l'oeil wainscoting. Whereas the uprights are treated in herringbone, the panels form trellis-work that is redolent, in the context of the luxuriant palm fronds nearby, of a winter garden.

**Above** On some straw matting and beneath a painted and distressed coffered ceiling extend the spaces of a small living and dining room. The cane furniture reflects the natural spirit of the locale. To the rear, the vast fireplace surround is composed of a sizable slab of carved marble in front of which shimmers the light from a blown-glass lamp. On the table, some old *suzanis* have been reinvented as a tablecloth. As demonstrated by the pyramid of oranges that rises like a precious article in barbotine slipcast decoration, the illusion of simplicity here achieves the perfect balance between a sense of naturalness and a total command of every decorative technique.

**Pages 238–239** In a peaceful interior patio, an alcove framed by the ornately carved columns in sweet-smelling cedarwood under a lintel hosts a bench almost submerged beneath cushions. To chest height, and all round the recess, where they are ornamented with a corolla of green cabochons, terracotta tiles present stripped-down rewrites of classic *zellige* motifs. Two impressive mosque lamps hang to either side of this restful corner, which remains refreshingly cool in all seasons.

**Facing page and right** Behind an old door, the way to a guest room resembling an imaginary Berber tent is signaled by a regular series of Moorish arches. The stripes painted on the walls recur on the ceiling in an optic effect that recreates the sky in fabric form. A modest straw-covered bench offers a graceful counterpoint to the embroidery on the garnet-red silk cushions, a color that reappears on a tablecloth and hems the curtains. An Orientalist canvas on the wall and a traditional folding stool on a soft-pile carpet complete a sober decor that exudes quality over quantity.

**Facing page and left** A further room with walls covered in yellow-tinged white *tadelakt* boasts richly carved and inlaid traditional furniture acquired in Egypt or Syria arranged beneath the wooden ceiling. An odalisque evoking the Orient of Matisse seems to gaze over to the bed; and indeed the throw made of *suzanis* looks very much like the cloth on which her form reclines. The adjacent bathroom opens onto the garden through traditional wooden shutters. Two horseshoe arches, the unfussy bands of *zellige*, and the walls in *tadelakt* seek to fuse a Western taste for sobriety with local techniques. When the shutters are thrown back, the desk with its finely worked old chair in front of the window is an ideal place to write and gaze out at the scene beyond. The color of the bouquet of bougainvillea seems to have been the source for the bands of fabric running round the foot of the voile curtains.

**Facing page and above** The gossamer
lightness of the lace on the wrought-iron
tester, the red-velvet upholstered bench,
and the small framed portrait on the bedside
table give this room, viewed through a
horseshoe arch a deliciously ex-colonial feel.
With disarming ease, Alberto Pinto has
composed a decorative ensemble of
unimpeachable authenticity. Conversing with
a naturalness and sincerity that is usually
acquired only through the passage of time,
this former farmhouse shows how to retie
the knot between the generations
of the past and those of the present.

**Left** In the light reflected from the celadon green walls with an enamel tile dado, this bedroom is appointed with a simplicity that seems to come from another world. The bed, with a gilt-copper baldachin, gives the room an old-fashioned air. Like some homely old country house, it teems with a haphazard amalgam of objects of all periods and from all places. Historic views of Naples, a mirror with a preciously ornate Oriental frame, cane chairs…. The bathroom is less reticent in its statement of local identity: Moorish arches and *zellige* partake of a tradition here reinterpreted to take account of Western comforts.

**Facing page** On a terrace on an upper floor of the house, a table with a stone mosaic top is surrounded by wicker chairs providing a setting for a leisurely breakfast or for a game between friends around an ice tea. Great pots of bougainvillea in flower luxuriate over the terracotta floor tiles. The inexhaustible visual pleasure afforded by such exuberant vegetation is not unlike the experience of exploring an interior by Alberto Pinto, where one's eye is forever lighting on some natural and self-evident detail one had previously failed to notice.

**Pages 250–251** As of 2010, at the Hôtel de la Victoire, from which radiates Alberto Pinto's creativity, the first Pinto Paris collection can be viewed by appointment.
The eclecticism of the furniture, presented in a dining room and living room space, allows the ornamental power of the object to flourish in this parade of individualized materials, techniques and forms. Here, with this collection of curiosities and works of art that evoke the rich inspiration of Brazil, the call to touch, the seduction of appearances, and the suggestion of comfort suddenly take precedence over function. A piece of furniture signed Alberto Pinto greatly exceeds its practical usage—it awakes emotion and sensibility.

# Singular Elements of Decoration

Every single project Alberto Pinto directs is exceptional. Each one is character-ized by an overriding preoccupation with exclusivity that is nourished at once by his clients' dreams and by the designer's ability to make them a reality and create *singular elements of decoration*. His fabrics, carpets, plates, etc. are all born in this manner, not forgetting the unique pieces of furniture whose ornamental qualities derive from their very structure.

From this plethora of original forms, today Alberto Pinto issues under the Pinto Paris brand a debut collection that aims to make his work available to a wider circle of admirers. It comes as an extension of the table services that have already been on the market for several years.

Manufactured by French craftsmen, this new line revels in underplayed mate-rial contrasts, sensual expression of comfort, and seductive details that reveal themselves only gradually. The product also makes use of some remarkable inno-vations, whose ingenuity is masked by the traditions of the most masterly workmanship. These glorious objects are born from a vast array of noble and sim-ple materials treated with time-honored techniques.

They embody the spirit of an untamable yet sophisticated city, where the old world and the new, where a luxuriant nature and high civilization live cheek by jowl. A Janus-like city that looks both over the Atlantic horizon and into the depths of the rainforest city whose infinitely inspiring marvels Alberto Pinto hails by christening his first collection "Rio."

**Facing page and left** Shown here in isolation or focusing on certain details, the objects signed Alberto Pinto display his taste for contrasting natural materials, the importance of comfort, as well as the absolute intransigence of the quality of his finish and effects. This leads him to go beyond the realm of interior design and decoration, to become a lifestyle designer for his clients, and allow their personality to blossom. This is achieved by personalizing and rigorously selecting all of the house linen, as well as in the pure creation of certain pieces of tableware necessary for the pleasure of the aesthete, as much as for the duties of presentation. His unique table services in Limoges porcelain, enhanced with the finesse of a drawing or painting exclusively done by hand, have been released over the last few years. Continuing and limited series are now on show in the second exhibition space of the Hôtel de la Victoire, where their meticulous style can be appreciated.

# Credits

| | |
|---|---|
| Cover | © Gerhard Richter 2010 |
| p. 8 | © Arman / Adagp, Paris 2010 |
| p. 12 | © The estate of Francis Bacon / All right reserved / Adagp, Paris 2010 |
| | © Gerhard Richter 2010 |
| p. 13 | © Gerhard Richter 2010 |
| p. 16 | © Zao Wou Ki / Adagp, Paris 2010 |
| | © Gerhard Richter 2010 |
| p. 17 | © Gerhard Richter 2010 |
| p. 18 | © Gerhard Richter 2010 |
| | © Max Ernst / Adagp, Paris 2010 |
| p. 21 | © Zao Wou Ki / Adagp, Paris 2010 |
| p. 22 | © Gerhard Richter 2010 |
| | © Max Ernst / Adagp, Paris 2010 |
| p. 24 | © Bernard Dufour / Adagp, Paris 2010 |
| p. 26 | © Lucio Fontana / Adagp, Paris 2010 |
| | © Serge Poliakoff / Adagp, Paris 2010 |
| | © John Michael Armleder |
| p. 27 | © Jan Fabre / Adagp, Paris 2010 |
| | © John Michael Armleder |
| p. 28 | © Anish Kapoor |
| | © Lucio Fontana / Adagp, Paris 2010 |
| | © Jan Fabre / Adagp, Paris 2010 |
| | © Miguel Berrocal / Adagp, Paris 2010 |
| p. 29 | © René Magritte / Adagp, Paris 2010 |
| p. 31 | © Manolo Valdès |
| | © Lucio Fontana / Adagp, Paris 2010 |
| p. 32 | © Max Ernst / Adagp, Paris 2010 |
| p. 34 | © Wim Delvoye / Adagp, Paris 2010 |
| | © Arman / Adagp, Paris 2010 |
| p. 35 | © Thomas Ruff |
| p. 38–39 | © Lenka Beillevert |
| p. 40 | *Flying Path 6*, 2009 © Lyndi Sales |
| p. 41 | © Jeff Kowatch |
| p. 42–43 | © Aki Kuroda / Adagp, Paris 2010 |
| | *Shatter, variation 3/5*, 2009 © Lyndi Sales |
| p. 44 | Série *Nudité*, 2008 © Marco Del Re |
| p. 45 | © Deborah Warshawski |
| p. 47 | *Substances abstraites I et II*, 2008 © Violaine Chevalier |
| p. 65 | *Hutington Beach*, 2006 © Raphaël Dautigny |
| p. 66 | © Mocanu |
| p. 70 | © Joan Miró © Successió Miró / Adagp, Paris 2010 |
| p. 72 | *Vase noire*, 2009 © Marco Del Re |
| p. 73 | © Joan Miró © Successió Miró / Adagp, Paris 2010 |
| p. 78 | © Raoul Ubac / Adagp, Paris 2010 |
| p. 98 | © Aki Kuroda / Adagp, Paris 2010 |
| p. 99 | © Dominique Derive |
| p. 102 | © Malevich |
| p. 103 | © Malevich |
| p. 108 | © Successió Miró / Adagp, Paris 2010 |
| p. 109 | © Successió Miró / Adagp, Paris 2010 |
| p. 112 | © Lenka Beillevert |
| p. 114–115 | © Lenka Beillevert |
| p. 118–119 | *les poissons de Monsieur H V*, 2003 © Marco Del Re |
| | *Undelig reise*, 2005 © Kjell Nupen / Adagp, Paris 2010 |
| | *Black/white tree 2*, 2003-04© Frode Steinicke / Adagp, Paris 2010 |
| | *Blue tree 2*, 2003-04 © Frode Steinicke / Adagp, Paris 2010 |
| p. 120 | *Idylle oubliée*, 2005 © Kjell Nupen / Adagp, Paris 2010 |
| p. 123 | *Landscape of my mind I*, 2005 © Vibeke Tojner |
| p. 124 | *Landscape of my mind I*, 2005 © Vibeke Tojner |
| p. 126 | *T-riffic*, 1966-67 © Allen Jones |
| p. 127 | *T-riffic*, 1966-67 © Allen Jones |
| p. 128 | *A concise history of aviation. Part 7*, 2004 © Ole Terslose |
| | *A concise history of aviation. Part 5*, 2004 © Ole Terslose |
| p. 130 | *Idylle oubliée*, 2005 © Kjell Nupen / Adagp, Paris 2010 |
| p. 132 | *Transformation*, 2002 © Lene Bodker |
| p. 133 | *Clay Creek*, 2003 © Bent Holstein |
| p. 136 | © Lucio Fontana / Adagp, Paris 2010 |
| p. 137 | © Lucio Fontana / Adagp, Paris 2010 |
| p. 138 | © Mimmo Rotella / Adagp, Paris 2010 |
| p. 141 | © Mimmo Rotella / Adagp, Paris 2010 |
| p. 143 | © César / Adagp, Paris 2010 |
| p. 144 | © César / Adagp, Paris 2010 |
| p. 154 | *Porte del sapere*, 2003 © Courtesy of Arnaldo Pomodoro |
| p. 156 | © Estate of Roy Lichtenstein New York / Adagp, Paris 2010 |
| p. 157 | © Édouard Vuillard / Adagp, Paris 2010 |
| p. 158 | © Pierre Bonnard /Adagp, Paris 2010 |
| p. 161 | © Succession Picasso 2010 |
| p. 162 | © The Andy Warhol Foundation for the Visual Arts, Inc. / Adagp, Paris 2010 |
| p. 163 | © Succession Picasso 2010 |
| p. 164 | © Egon Schiele |
| p. 165 | © Egon Schiele |
| p. 166–167 | © Alexandre Fassianos |
| p. 177 | *Nu blanc*, 2002 © Marco Del Re |
| p. 179 | *Compotier blanc*, 1998 © Marco Del Re |
| p. 185 | © Marc du Plantier |
| | © François-Xavier Lalanne / Adagp, Paris 2010 |
| p. 200 | *Up* © Anna Skibska |
| p. 202 | *Up* © Anna Skibska |
| p. 213 | © Mimmo Rotella / Adagp, Paris 2010 |
| p. 218 | *The Pont Neuf Wrapped, Project for Paris* (detail), 1985 © Christo 1985 |
| p. 221 | © Amando Tanzini |
| | *Composition*, 2002 © Sofia Vari |
| p. 224 | © De Chirico / Adagp, Paris 2010 |
| p. 250 | Alexander Calder © Calder Foundation New York / Adagp, Paris 2010 |

The editor and publisher gratefully acknowledge the permission granted to reproduce the copyright material in this book. Every effort has been made to trace copyright holders and to obtain their permission for the use of copyright material. The publisher apologizes for any errors or omissions in the above list and would be grateful if notified of any corrections that should be incorporated in future reprints or editions of this book.

**Photographic credits:** Ph. © Jacques Pépion: p. 2, 4, 8, 9, 10, 12, 13, 14, 15, 16, 17, 18, 19, 20, 21, 22, 23, 24, 26, 27, 28, 29, 30, 31, 32, 33, 34, 35, 36, 38, 39, 40, 41, 42, 43, 44, 45, 46, 47, 48, 50, 51, 52, 53, 54, 55, 56, 57, 58, 59, 60, 62, 63, 64, 65, 66, 67, 68, 69, 70, 71, 72, 73, 74, 75, 76, 77, 78, 79, 80, 82, 83, 84, 85, 86, 87, 88, 89, 90, 91, 92, 93, 94, 95, 112, 114, 115, 116, 117, 118, 119, 120, 121, 122, 123, 124, 125, 126, 127, 128, 129, 130, 131, 132, 133, 146, 148, 149, 150, 151, 152, 153, 168, 170, 171, 172, 173, 174, 175, 176, 177, 178, 179, 180, 181, 182, 184, 185, 186, 187, 188, 189, 190, 191, 192, 193, 194, 195, 196, 197, 198, 199, 200, 202, 203, 204, 205, 206, 207, 208, 210, 211, 212, 213, 214, 215, 216, 217, 218, 219, 220, 221, 222, 223, 224, 225, 226, 228, 229, 230, 231, 232, 233, 234, 235, 236, 237, 238, 239, 240, 241, 242, 243, 244, 245, 246, 247, 248, 250, 251, 252, 253, 254
Ph. © Vanessa von Zitzewitz: p. 7
Ph. © Giorgio Baroni: p. 8, 9, 96, 98, 99, 100, 101, 102, 103, 104, 105, 106, 107, 108, 109, 110, 111, 134, 136, 137, 138, 139, 140, 141, 142, 143, 144, 145, 154, 156, 157, 158, 159, 160, 161, 162, 163, 164, 165, 166, 167

# Acknowledgments

Julien Morel thanks Benoît Chottin and the team at Maison Alberto Pinto for their invaluable guidance.
Thanks also to Laurent Denize d'Estrées and to the 14 Septembre Agency for their support, and to Aurélia Maillard for her unwavering devotion.

JULIEN MOREL
After studying history of art,
Julien Morel became a lifestyle
and design writer. He now works
for a leading communications
and PR agency in Paris.

OTHER ALBERTO PINTO TITLES
Alberto Pinto *Classics*
Alberto Pinto *Moderns*
Alberto Pinto *Orientalism*
Alberto Pinto *Bedrooms*
Alberto Pinto *Corporate*
Alberto Pinto *Table Settings*

**MAISON ALBERTO PINTO**
SHOW ROOM PINTO PARIS
11, rue d'Aboukir – 75002 Paris
Tél. : +33 (0) 1 40 13 00 00
Fax : +33 (0) 1 40 13 75 80
www.pintoparis.com www.albertopinto.com

Editorial Director: Ghislaine Bavoillot
Translated from the French by David Radzinowicz
Design: Isabelle Ducat
Copyediting: Kay Hyman
Typesetting: Claude-Olivier Four
Proofreading: Marc Feustel
Color Separation: Reproscan, Bergamo
Printed in Italy by Canale

Simultaneously published in French as *Alberto Pinto Inédits*
© Flammarion, S.A., Paris, 2010

English-language edition
© Flammarion, S.A., Paris, 2010

editions.flammarion.com

10 11 12   3 2 1

ISBN: 978-2-08-020074-7

Dépôt légal: 10/2010